Dedication

I dedicate this book to all the people of **God** who live in the Holy City; the over-comers, survivors, the mighty, the weak, the victors and the victims, those who are battling secretly and silently.

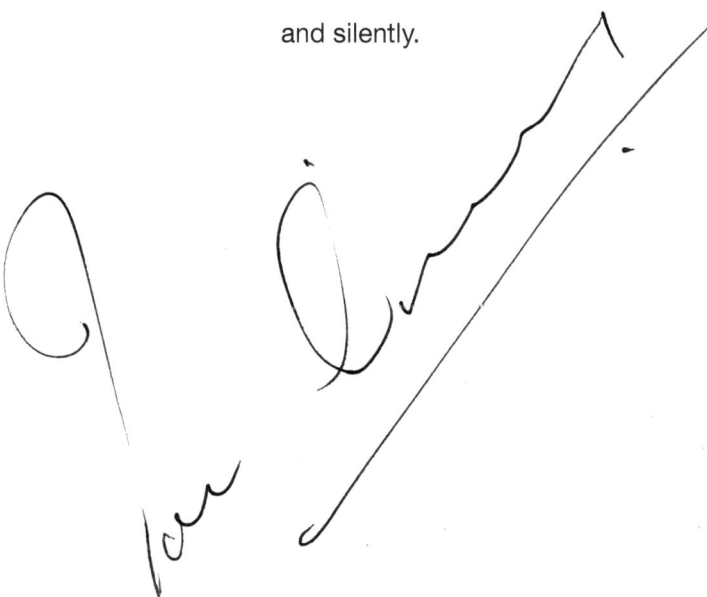

Contents

Acknowledgements	3
Editor's Review	5
Introduction	6
A Tale of Two Cities	11
There's a Hit on Your Life	24
There's a Harlot in the House	36
Jezebel, the Political Harlot	41
Delilah, the Professional	54
Tamar, the Opportunist	61
One Night Stand	72
Married to a Stripper	77
Controlling Your Appetite	81
What About You?	125
Practical Guidelines	146

Acknowledgements

First I will like to thank God for sustaining me, keeping me and covering me through the writing of this book. The wisdom and revelation, trials, testing and temptations made the journey a very interesting one.

Also, thanks to my wife Lana T Cummings for her patience and understanding through the years of attacks and trials which came because of the assignment and the mandate of ROTA.

Thanks to my father Rev. Isaiah E. Cummings and mother Pearl Cummings; my brothers and sisters and the entire Empowerment Temple International family. Thanks to my daughters Kereen I. and Anya G. Cummings as well as my son David Hawthorne.

To my spiritual sons and daughters across the globe that God has allowed me to spiritually birth, mentor and cover, thank you. To Prophet Juliette Van Zoolingen and to Melvin Molhoop, I say thanks. To my covering Bishop E. Benn and Dr. Delores Benn, I am truly grateful for you both.

Thanks to Keris Ramkaran and Minister Wilt Bernard for being there through the years of the birthing forth of this ROTA and Sex in the City.

To my mentor and father Apostle Cassiaus Farrell, I extend much gratitude for your divine connection and the impact you will continue to have on my mind. Being attached to you has changed my entire life.

I am grateful for a daughter, a mentee and a friend - the author of "Being a Virgin Isn't Enough" (BAVIE) - Chadia Mathurin. Much love and thanks for your input, dedication and openness.

Overall, to my intercessors such as Pastor Leslie-Ann Byron - her stand for holiness and purity is like no other; and all the people who believed in me, I say thanks.

Editor's Review

It was quite the journey working on this book but at the end of it, I felt proud to have had my part to play in this piece. This book is very unique in its content and intent. Never before has anyone come out to address this issue the way the author does in his exposition and explanation of biblical characters, events and subsequent implications.

The parallels to the church made within these pages are astounding and as I read I can see the reality of the situations playing out daily. It is truly amazing how biblical accounts have substantial bearing on activities in the Church today. As you read, open your mind and your spirit and you too will see truth coming out in everything shared here on sexual perversion.

Editor Cherisse Forde

Introduction

If the title of this book drew you, it was my intention, but we will not in any way discuss the television series. Rather, my aim is to disclose facts of an underlying issue in our churches for years now – sexual immorality among leaders and congregants of churches, who profess Christ.

This publication will give you information to help you understand how the Heathen City (the world) has infiltrated the Holy City (the Church), the effects of such and how the Holy City can be guarded and purged of the sexual perversion that is now prevalent.

When people think of the Church in its ideal state, they think of purity, holiness and "rightness." They do not think of the Church as an environment within which issues concerning sex and sexuality are mentioned or can be adequately discussed. They think how on earth am I going to discuss my sex life with my pastor or my brothers and sisters in Christ in this sanctuary? How can I guard myself against sexual sins? What happens if I am a Christian who has indulged in sexual sin?

In recent times, the Church has been under tremendous attacks, conflict, and scrutiny as a result of an increase in sexually immoral behavior. In light of the influx of global news reports on sexual immorality within the Church, one would assume that a blind eye has been turned to every Scripture written on the topic. September of last year, a Catholic Archbishop was arrested after over 100,000 pornographic images were found on his computer. His predecessor was arrested on charges that he paid a number of minors to have sex with him between 2008 and 2012.

The worst part is that there is an ongoing debate as to whether Protestant churches or Catholic churches are guiltier of sexual immorality. This should not even be a debate associated with the Church yet it is very real. On an almost daily basis, there are pastors performing sexual acts outside their marriages. In Atlanta, Georgia, one pastor was accused of spreading HIV to many women. Other pastors have been hit with allegations of homosexual relationships, child molestation, and every other imaginable sexual sin. It leaves one to wonder that since those in the fore of the Church struggle so severely with issues of sexual immorality, if the Church will ever come to a proper understanding of sex.

If the Church cannot come into an understanding of sex, will the world ever be rightly influenced where sex is concerned? When would anyone have imagined sexual sins would become so prevalent among those who claim to be in better standing with God than others because of their righteous lifestyles? The reality is that while these issues are not unique to the 21st Century City (the Church), it is unique to find men and women of God who will venture into the waters that require them to candidly discuss sex in the City. It is like the Star Trek of Christianity – *"Going where no man has ever gone before!"*

I believe that God has raised me up as one who will dive head first into these waters. God has given me certain revelations about certain sexual practices and spirits that are of a foreign and unclean City (the world) and has armed me with a mandate to expose how the enemy is using sexual immorality to usurp His City. Many people doubt the relevance of the Bible when it comes to addressing the issues of modern life. Nonetheless, as will be evident from later examples, the sexual issues that this book aims to address have existed since the days of the Old Testament. The problems are not new, neither are the solutions.

The citizens of God's Holy City must avoid defiling themselves through sexually immoral behavior. When sexually immoral behavior exists within the boundaries of the Church, those armed with discernment will recognize the fruits of it, and when these fruits are recognized, there must be a pruning of that which produces such fruit in order to avoid the continued growth of this dangerous ulcer. It is not as simple as that though; there are many dynamics at play in the arena of sexual perversion by Christians.

For many who go through sexual struggles in the Church, this book should be able to clear up the reason why you are being attacked. While reading it, though, you may notice that the attack is intensifying in your life. Remember the devil wants to bring you down even before you get into a leadership position. That way, when you have risen to meet that position, he has a way of making you fall and keeping you in his pit. Once he sinks his claws into you, they are hard to remove. You will still feel the pain of the scars once they are gone.

This book also equips you with the understanding of sexual urges and how to manage them along with many other helpful tips on this topic. So take this short journey with me as we uncover Sex in the City.

ROTA - SEX IN THE CITY

CHAPTER ONE

[A TALE OF TWO CITIES]

From the genesis of the Bible, a distinction has been made between two cities: good and evil, God's people and those who were not His, light and darkness, the Church and the world, the hot and the cold. The distinction between these cities was made clear by the differences in their practices. One City was characterized by holiness, purity, pleasing God, and truth, while the other was characterized by evil, sexual immorality, pleasing the enemy, lies and deception. For the purpose of this book, we will identify and distinguish these two cities as the Holy City and the Heathen City.

The Holy City.

"Ye are the salt of the earth: but if the salt have lost his savour, wherewith shall it be salted? It is thenceforth good for nothing, but to be cast out, and to be trodden under foot of men. Ye are the light of the world. A city that is set on an hill cannot be hid. Neither do men light a candle, and put it under a bushel, but on a candlestick; and it giveth light unto all that are in the house. Let your light so shine before men, that they may see your good works, and glorify your Father which is in heaven."

- Matthew 5:13-16 (KJV)

The Holy City is the Church and it is representative of God's ways. It is a manifestation of God's will and order of His Church. In the Holy City, God is worshipped in Spirit and in truth, and the people of this City follow carefully His instructions for every facet of life.

It is told in the book of Matthew that where marriage is concerned, a man is expected to cleave to his wife. The English words "to cleave" are denoted by the word proskollao in the Hebrew text; meaning to adhere to or to glue. In ancient times, marriage within the Holy City was more than just the wedding, the feasting and a marriage certificate. A very pivotal part of marriage was consummation (sexual intercourse). It was only at the point of consummation that a man and woman were truly considered husband and wife. The point of consummation denoted the point where the man and the woman became "one flesh" and - in many ways - one person.

From this, we glean that sex is not something that God takes lightly. Sexual intercourse is the means by which a man and a woman achieve the spiritual aim of marriage: the oneness. It would therefore be accurate to say that sexual intercourse is the physical correspondence to the spiritual joining of the entities that engage in the said act.

God's will for this City is not only that it exerts influence on the Heathen City, but that it overpowers the Heathen City. When "overpowering" takes place, that which is subject does not, in any way, control or influence that which is master. As such, the Holy City would be able to exert influence without becoming a part of the Heathen City.

In Matthew Chapter 5, Jesus refers to the Holy City as the "light of the world" and "salt of the earth." When light enters a space of darkness, it eliminates darkness. However, if darkness enters a space that is lit, it cannot expel light. In the same way, when salt touches its subject, its subject becomes salty, but salt never takes on the flavor of its subject. Thus, these comparisons have very important implications for how the Holy City should function in any sphere – including sexual matters. Unfortunately, this is not always the case!

> **The Heathen City.**
>
> *The Heathen City is the world and it is representative of the devil's ways. It is a manifestation of all contaminated versions of the sex. The Heathen City is characterized by fornication, pornography, masturbation, adultery, etc. In the Heathen City, the occupants do whatever they wish, whenever they wish and however they wish to. It is governed by something called humanism where persons are encouraged to do whatever feels good. The Scripture that comes to mind out of this mentality is:*
>
> *"In those days there was no king in Israel, but every man did that which was right in his own eyes."*
>
> *- Judges 17:6 (KJV)*

Only that the Heathen City does have a king – Satan.

When the Heathen City Enters the Holy City.

Numbers 22 records that the Holy City was functioning in the way which God intended for it to function and that it overpowered any Heathen City in its vicinity. The Moabites had heard of the power of Israel (a type of the Church), and they were in fear that they would experience the same fate previously experienced by the Amorites. The Moabite leader, Balak, was with due reason, very afraid. He believed that the only solution to the problem of Israel was to place a curse upon the children of Israel, and so he sent his messengers to solicit the aid of the ever efficient diviner Balaam.

The consequent verses show that God instructed Balaam not to curse the Israelites and despite Balak's insistence and persistence to make available to him tremendous physical gain, Balaam subjected himself to the order of God. The order of God was to continually bless Israel in lieu of Balak's continual insistence to curse the Holy City. It is therefore evident that when the Israelites were in covenant with God, and they followed His precepts it was impossible for infiltration or defeat to occur. They were unstoppable; they were tremendously blessed by the hand of God, and overpowered every foreign city in war. But, somewhere around Numbers 25, we see the people of the Holy City coming into an experience quite contrary to their norm of victory, life, health and prosperity.

> *"And the Lord said unto Moses, Take all the heads of the people, and hang them up before the Lord against the sun, that the fierce anger of the Lord may be turned away from Israel. And Moses said unto the judges of Israel, Slay ye every one of his men that was joined unto Baal-peor. And those that died in the plague were twenty and four thousand."*
>
> - Numbers 25: 1-4, 9 (KJV)

What could possibly have caused God to turn His back on His beloved people? How is it that a nation under a covenant of tremendous favor with God, experience the death of thousands of its people at the hands of a plague? The answer lays in the verses preceding Numbers 25:9: The Seduction of Israel by Moab.

> *"And Israel abode in Shittim, and the people began to commit whoredom with the daughters of Moab. And they called the people unto the sacrifices of their Gods: and the people did eat, and bowed to their gods. And Israel joined himself unto Baal-peor: and the anger of the Lord was kindled against Israel. And, behold one of the children of Israel came and brought unto his brethren a Midianite woman in the sight of Moses, and in the sight of all the congregation of Israel, who were weeping before the door of the tabernacle of the congregation."*
>
> - Numbers 25:1-3, 6 (KJV)

Moab (The Heathen City) was unsuccessful in its first strategic attempt to seize and defeat Israel via the medium of divination. But there were other strategies. The new strategy was defined by self-defeat; Israel would fall out of covenant and favor with God, not because of divination but because of sexual perversion.

The interactions between Israel and Moab are a mirror image of the interactions between the present day Church and the ruler of the world. The ruler of the world often tries to dismantle the Church using several strategies, but most times its success is found in the strategy of the seduction of the Church, defined by deception and the infiltration of sexual immorality.

In the 21st century, more often than not, we hear how sexual perversion brings down the man in the spotlight, discrediting the Church as a whole. This is also a parallel drawn from the record in Numbers 25. The name of the Israelite man was Zimri. The name derived from the word group zamar (a Hebrew word for praise) and can find its English translation in the phrases, "my music," "my praise" or "my musician." Thus, this makes reference to God's music, God's praise and God's musician.

An examination of the meaning behind the name ***"Cozbi"*** will further bring enlightenment to this parallel.

The name Cozbi comes from the Hebrew verb kazab, making reference to a lie, a falsehood, or deception. The joining of Zimri and Cozbi is therefore interpreted as an intercourse between God's music, God's praise, God's musician and a lie, falsehood, or deception. It therefore becomes evident that part of the enemy's strategic scheme involves a targeting of God's praise and those who carry it, by lies, falsehood and deception.

Furthermore, we find that sexual perversion in the Church is not something carried out in secrecy or seclusion. Men and women have come into boldness in their defiance of the precepts of God, and now, more than ever, the presence of sexual perversion is brought into the sanctuary, on the pulpit, and in the choir. Just as the Israelite man brought the Midianite woman to his tent in the presence of the congregation, so too have men and women of the Church boldly and unashamedly brought sexual impurities into the Church.

Despite the seeming graveness of this mirroring, the pointing out of these parallels between the deliberate plan of the Moabites and the intentional nature of the enemy (the devil) does not serve the purpose of bringing the Church into a state of hopelessness where the topic of sexual immorality is concerned. Just as we have drawn parallels with the Moabite's calculated actions and that of the enemy, we can also draw parallels between how Israel came into a restoration of God's favor after the stench of sexual perversion, and how the Church can come into restoration of God's favor after it has been infiltrated by sexual sins.

> *"And when Phinehas, the son of Eleazar, the son of Aaron the priest, saw it, he rose up from among the congregation, and took a javelin in his hand; And he went after the man of Israel into the tent, and thrust both of them through, the man of Israel, and the woman through her belly. So the plague was stayed from the children of Israel."*
>
> - Numbers 25:7-8 (KJV)

For too long, the Church has remained silent; not addressing the scourge of sexual immorality, providing reasons ranging from the need for political correctness and extending mercy to those involved as opposed to condemning them. Whatever the Church's reasons for taking a lackadaisical approach in addressing this issue in its pews and on its pulpits, the account given in Numbers seems to be in stark disagreement with its stance.

The ancient tale of the two cities exposed in Numbers 22-25 teaches us that the presence of distorted sexuality within the Holy City is not to be tolerated. Sexual immorality amongst the people of the Holy City angers God. For the sake of the restoration of favor and the advancement of the City into the promises of God, there must be a cleansing or purge.

Are we therefore called to pierce the bellies of all involved in sexual immorality within the Church with spears? The dispensation of grace which presently guides the Church does not call for the physical use of spears; neither does it call for any form of apathy or acceptance of such sins. It calls for the use of the spiritual spear (deliverance) and it calls for a piercing of the spiritual womb.

You see, the record of Phinehas' actions was not without great significance. The account tells us that Phinehas plunged a spear in both the man and woman's belly. The belly is the home of the womb, and the spiritual womb is the incubator for unclean spirits. Phinehas was in a sense, delivering someone of the Holy City from an unclean spirit marked by sexual impurity. Unfortunately, during the Levitical period, deliverance was marked by death of the physical body which carried the unclean spirit.

The description of Phinehas is also important to the understanding of deliverance. It was made clear that Phinehas was from the lineage of priesthood. In the Old Testament, someone would fulfill this requirement if they hailed from the lineage of Aaron, but in this new dispensation of grace, through the shedding of the blood of the Lamb of God, we have all been accorded the authority of the priest.

Therefore, it is to be noted that both during the period of legality and the period of grace that the priest must hold a stature of purity. Righteousness and purity have always been God's desire for His children and continues to be. God expects the Church to abstain from sexual immorality and all other sins. How can we uphold this standard? Now that we understand the differences between the Church and the world, we can look at our lives in perspective.

ROTA - SEX IN THE CITY

CHAPTER TWO

[THERE'S A HIT ON MY LIFE]

It is often said that there are two sets of plans for a human being – God's plan and the enemy's plan. The moment an individual is born, there are demonic forces trying to get him/her to veer away from God's plan for his/her life. Biblical characters were not exempted. Throughout the Bible, we see accounts of the enemy using sexual immorality to destroy several men of purpose and we see those who resisted.

One of the aims and objectives of the enemy is to bring down the mighty men and women of God, those who have been given an extremely great responsibility and call upon their lives. And because of this, the attacks, the approach and the tactics of the enemy are unique to the target.

It was soon after I received my call to full time ministry that the Lord spoke to me through a dream in which I was being pursued by demonic forces. When I awoke, it was so real that I was sweating profusely and marks were made on my skin. I immediately asked the Lord the meaning of the dream and he led me to the book of Judges, particularly the account with Sampson and Delilah.

He told me to study it because there was a hit on my life and the enemy wanted to make sure that I aborted my mission and never fulfill my purpose. He also revealed that there were people who were in bondage and captivity, waiting for what I am carrying so the enemy wanted to stop me. Once you step into the Lord's work, the enemy gets mad at you. He does not want you teaching and preaching the Word. So, he puts out a hit on your life.

He will do all that is necessary to destroy your ministry. If there is a hit on my life, then there is going to be a hit man. A hit man is a trained assassin who is a professional at putting people out of commission. This professional is paid and appointed to terminate your life. In the world, hit men usually work for organizations that are political or criminal in nature.

However, just as the enemy has a hit on your life, God has a wonderful plan for your life. While the enemy is planning you defeat, God is planning your success. God has a purpose for your destiny, but if we are not aware of the enemy's devices, we will find ourselves trapped and falling short of accomplishing the mission we have received from God. We may even be forced to abort it instead of fulfilling the purpose for our lives.

At this time we focus on two very popular men in the Bible and see how their lives were mapped out but later sabotaged, all surrounding sexual perversion.

SAMSON

Judges 13-16 and 21-30 outlines the life of Samson. Samson was a judge divinely appointed to rescue Israel from the hand of the Philistines, but his weakness was his prodigious appetite for women. The record shows that the lords of the Philistines employed several strategies to defeat their rival including the use of women. Their final attempt which proved to be successful was the enchanting Delilah. Delilah's achievement of distracting Samson ended in the abortion of his purpose and destiny.

God had spoken to Samson's parents concerning how they were to raise him. Although he was gifted to deliver Israel out of bondage, he never quite lived up to his call. In part, this may have arisen from the problem that he stepped into the dimension of his calling before his time. From the time he was little, he had been told he was special and he would deliver his people from oppression.

He went about it the wrong way, because certain dimensions of his life were not fully developed. He did not step into a life of true strength, because he had not developed the maturity necessary for the task. Instead, he entered his ministry while he was still frivolous and flaky. When you step into ministry before your time, without the proper training and covering, it can lead to disaster.

You must be accountable to someone and that person must be able to speak into your life to tell you if you are going wrong and when you need to sit and take a rest. Samson had no one to whom he was accountable. His parents allowed him to do as he wished and if he did something they did not approve of, they did not try to prevent him from doing it. Lack of accountability aided in his failed destiny since he ended up having to abort it prematurely.

Notice Samson's parents understood his spiritual calling, and made sure he knew who he was (a Nazarite). They informed him that he was special before the Lord, but perhaps this is why Samson seemed to live recklessly. When we look at the Church we see many problems where the sons and daughters are not willing to submit to the authority of the fathers and/or leaders. This is a real breakdown in the spiritual foundation of the Church.

Samson was about to war against a major principality of that time and confront a system that held the people of God captive for 40yrs; everything about his life was supposed to reflect moral uprightness. But he had a moral deficiency in that he was hurt and wanted vengeance. He started 'dating down' whereby he became unequally yoked. He was physically strong but spiritually light; he was impulsive.

The strength of Samson was in his vow of consecration not in his locks of hair; his power was in his sanctification, not his muscles. The further he drifted, the more difficult it became to keep the vow. His strength was still there, but his commitment wavered. Strength cannot keep us, but commitment to God can.

If God is calling you to deliver people or has a specific task for you to accomplish or a particular assignment, your walk must be different; you will be set apart, you will be able to do things the average person will not. You cannot hang out in the same places as others, you cannot associate closely with the same people as others, and you cannot commit the same acts as others. You must be guarded for your purpose.

Delilah was not just any woman; she represents a spirit that feeds on the men's lust. The spirit behind Delilah, as we will see later, functions when men without strength and governmental authority are around. There will be no Delilah if there were no men with dysfunctional morals. She was a harlot with a contract; an assassin.

She had a mission, a target, a name and an agenda. There was a hit on Samson's life and he didn't know. She wants to sell her spirit and uses her body to bargain.

There is a hit on your life, not necessarily because of whom you are but who you are connected to. Being connected to Jesus means we are drafted into a war that has nothing to do with us. Delilah's commitment was to take Samson's strength.

Samson was hurt and lost his vision so he was already weak. She is not bothered with your assignment, it's your vision and strength she is after. She has studied your actions and knows there is a secret to your success. You can never complete your assignment if your vision is blurred or your strength is shaky, so she strikes where it matters most.

The Philistines told Delilah *to entice him and find the secret of his strength*. There are some things the devil can't do in your life, your family and your community, but his aim is to be able to have free reign. The devil sends a demon cleverly trained to deal with your issue. They tried before and failed so they chose the best, to hit him at his weakest.

Samson was in love with Delilah and was already falling apart. She comforted him, and then wore him down. They took out his eyes so he would have no vision. Indeed, I can tell you that renewed vision and restoration came out of the situation and thus we ought to use our renewed strength to push and accomplish our task.

DAVID

1 Samuel to Hosea as well as Matthew, Mark and Acts reference a man named David who was one of Israel's most well-known and accomplished kings. As a warrior king, he was a force to be reckoned with and the Bible records him being called, by God "a man after my own heart" (see Acts 13:22). With all that he had going for him, it is no wonder that the enemy tried to take him out on several occasions.

Eventually, the enemy's triumphant weapon was Bathsheba. The moment an individual makes a decision to walk in the kingdom of light, he/she has entered a place of immense divine purpose. He/she must also understand that there are forces that are displeased with this decision and as such will stop at nothing to destroy that purpose.

David was a young boy when God ordained him to be King. He was the youngest of his brothers and seemingly the smallest; almost the forgotten son. When God's servant came to anoint him, his father called all his sons, but none of them was to be King and when asked if there was anyone else, he remembered David. When he slew Goliath they were all amazed, but he was already chosen by God for greatness. He grew and took his place as King, but also became an adulterer.

Many people wonder how God can call such a sinful man like David "a man after my own heart" but it rested in David's humility and response to his sin. Upon making mistakes, David hastily and eagerly sought God's forgiveness, but was always left with the bitter consequences. Truth be told, all have sinned and fallen short of the glory of God, but we must be responsible for our actions. We have hope in Christ to be forgiven and have our sins forgotten by Him, but the burdens we carry from these sins at times are not worth it.

David simply had one look at Bathsheba and it was all over. The Bible isn't wrong to caution us against the lust of the eyes because the eyes are the avenue through which much of the ills in our spirit enter. A simple look caused an anointed man grave trouble. Similarly, pornography is dangerous, it's not what the eyes see, that's the problem, it's the fact that it informs our thoughts and in an unguarded moment even our actions can be controlled by it.

Both Samson and David's sexual immorality altered every area of their lives. Samson's failure led to his death. It is said that he killed more Philistines in his death than when he was alive. What God could have done with his righteous life had to be accomplished in his sinful state, upon his death. Additionally, God could have done so much more with him if his life wasn't shortened by his own folly. The sin robbed him of the glory God had laid up for him.

The steep price of David's failure was adversity in his home, public humiliation, the death of his son and 70,000 Israelites and a falling away from the favor of God. David was no regular man you see; he was ordained by God, blessed by God and ruler over others. David demonstrates for us that, what Goliath could not do on the battlefield one look at a woman could do. It shows us what a man can kill on the battlefield and what can kill the man off the battlefield.

Sometimes we look at others and think they get away with their sin, but there is always a penalty, more so for those in the Body of Christ because we have the Word as our guide and we are representatives of God. The truth emphasized in this book is that there are spirits assigned to take out God's representatives and if we are not vigilant, anyone can fall prey to their devices.

ROTA - SEX IN THE CITY

CHAPTER THREE

[THERE'S A HARLOT IN THE HOUSE]

In Chapter One, we concluded that when sexual perversion or sexual spirits exist in the Church, they must be purged out. In recognition of this reality, this chapter will seek to provide more information on the spirits behind the scourge of sexual perversion in the Church. It is my experience that emphasis is often placed on the sexual acts as opposed to the spirits behind them. Our approach to the subject plays a significant role in our effectiveness in dealing with sexual immorality within the Church.

Careful consideration of Scripture will show that there are two major spirits of sexual immorality operating in the Body of Christ. I call these the "Harlot Spirit" and the *"Jezebel Spirit."* Although I refer to these spirits using feminine names and terms, these Spirits affect both men and women, following the understanding that spirits are gender neutral.

I will hereafter focus on the *"Harlot Spirit,"* showing Biblical examples of both men and women who have been affected by this spirit. But first, we will intrinsically examine the nature and operations of this spirit.

An Introduction to the Spirit of Harlotry.

A harlot is any woman, married or single, who practices unlawful sexual indulgence for material gain or for pleasure. The word *"harlot"* may describe intent rather than character and can be branded by an ironic combination of passivity and strength. This spirit is deceptively encouraging and supportive, and it sometimes lurks in the shadows waiting for opportune times. These opportune times revolve around the target's distress.

The Types of Harlots.

The Political Harlot: The political harlot is attracted to power, authority, leadership, and control. It therefore targets those in leadership and functions effectively through those who seek power. It uses sex to lure those in positions of authority away from God.

It constantly seeks ways to increase its influence. Jezebel is a prime example of a political harlot. She was never satisfied with the extension of the reins of power given to her by Ahab. She continuously sought more power, and simultaneously cut the people of Israel off from God in her quest.

The Professional Harlot: The professional harlot serves the purpose of bringing down the 'strong man.' This type of harlot presents its self as an answer to the fulfillment of the target's appetites. Because of its professionalism this harlot is persistent in the fulfillment of its objectives. This very persistence will exhaust the target, placing him/her in a place of spiritual blindness which will in turn lead him/her to reveal the source of his/her strength.

The professional harlot does not necessarily crave power, but will work for a particular price, and its mission *is to get the job done.* Delilah is representative of the professional harlot. She was sent on assignment as an exploitation of Samson's weakness and through persistence she got him to reveal the source of his strength.

The Opportunistic Harlot: The opportunistic harlot is not characterized by patience in as much as it is characterized by swiftness. This harlot values the limitations of time and the produced missteps of limited thought, operating with the aim of pushing one into making a bad decision. As the name implies, this harlot is an exploiter of circumstance; she is an *"opportunity grabber"*. Tamar is the opportunistic harlot, since she used circumstances and time to gain her heart's desire – a male heir.

These three women and the spirit of harlotry working with them did a great deal of damage to the lives of these significant men. The women may no longer exist, but this spirit of harlotry scans the earth, even today seeking to destroy men and women on fire for God. Let's look at them more closely.

ROTA - SEX IN THE CITY

CHAPTER FOUR

[JEZEBEL, THE POLITICAL HARLOT]

> *"And it came to pass, as if it had been a light thing for him to walk in the sins of Jeroboam the son of Nebat, that he took to wife Jezebel the daughter of Ethbaal king of the Zidonians, and went and served Baal, and worshipped him. He reared up an altar for Baal... which he had built in Samaria... And Ahab also made a grove; and Ahab did more to provoke the Lord, God of Israel, to anger than all the kings before him."*
>
> -1 Kings 16:31-33(KJV)

This label is assigned to Jezebel because of the sphere in which she operated. She moved within a sphere that included kings, prophets and priests, all of whom held positions of power. She was a woman known for imposing her will on others. Through calculation and ruthlessness she led the people of Israel away from God through sexual perversion and idolatry.

The spirit of harlotry as represented by Jezebel's life served the purpose of both the corruption and elimination of God's leadership, and God's ways and practices, all of which unconsciously resulted in the unfaithfulness and corruption of the congregation of Israel.

Jezebel is made mention of twice in the Bible; firstly in 1 Kings and second, in the book of Revelation. Neither of the accounts portrays her in a positive light. Jezebel became an intricate part of the fabric of Israel when Ahab married her, as confirmation for a political arrangement between the Zidonians and the northern kingdom of Israel.

As someone who followed the worship customs of Zidonia, Jezebel worshipped pagan gods, primarily Baal, the storm god, and Ashtoreth, the fertility goddess. Throughout her time in Israel it seemed that a large part of her actions were fueled by her desire to give Baal pre-eminence. The Bible does not tell us through what means, but we glean that Jezebel exerted a considerable measure of influence over Ahab.

Jezebel convinced Ahab to worship and build altars to Baal, he allowed her to take what did not belong to her, and he allowed her to execute the prophets of God, which in turn led to the worship of Baal by all of Israel, except 7,000. In the end, we see the children of Israel suffer for Ahab's weak leadership, and their unfaithfulness to God. The land suffered severe drought and desolation. Jezebel was highly strategic in achieving her aim.

There was no need to directly target the populace of Israel when targeting those in authority would have achieved the same result of giving Baal pre-eminence in the land of Israel. That which affected leadership eventually trickled down to the subjects. Her strategy was to focus on the corruption and extermination of leadership which resulted in the shutting down of revelation, increased sexual perversion, taking possession and bringing drought and desolation upon the land.

In the same way, when Jezebel is in the house there will be signs of corrupt leadership and congregation such as revelation being shut down, there will be an increase in sexual perversion, possessions will be taken from those in the Church and the congregation will experience a time of severe drought and desolation, all at the hands of this political harlot. As each of the results of Jezebel's actions is examined you will see how these happenings are also affecting the present-day Church.

Revelation is Shut Down

> *"For it was so, when Jezebel cut off the prophets of the Lord, that Obadiah took an hundred prophets, and hid them by fifty in a cave, and fed them with bread and water."*
>
> -1 Kings 18:4 (KJV)

When Jezebel sought to exterminate the prophets of God, it resulted in the shutdown of revelation in the land of Israel. After Elijah carried the people to the mount for a "showdown of the gods," and the prophets of Ba-al were killed, she threatened Elijah's life. She would tolerate no one speaking on behalf of the God of Israel, nor would she tolerate anyone speaking against Ba-al.

In the same way, when Jezebel is in the house, there will be signs of shady leadership. Even more, there will be forces at work seeking to silence the source of any truth and like Elijah, those who hold truth may be forced to move away for the sake of preservation. This will result in a tainted congregation likely to fall into behaviors that characterize unfaithfulness to God.

Sexual Perversion Increases.

Because of the gods which took pre-eminence in her life, sexual perversion and Jezebel were a package. Sexual perversion was the means by which these foreign gods brought to Israel by this harlot, were worshipped.

> *"And to the angel of the church in Thyatira write... I know thy works, and charity, and service, and faith and thy patience; and thy works; and the last to be more than the first. Notwithstanding, I have a few things against thee, because thou sufferest that woman Jezebel, which calleth herself a prophetess, to teach and to seduce my servants to commit fornication, and to eat things sacrificed unto idols. And I gave her space to repent of her fornication; and she repented not. Behold, I will cast her into a bed, and them that commit adultery with her into great tribulation, except they repent of their deeds... I will give unto every one of you according to your works."*
>
> – Revelation 2:18-23 (KJV)

In the book of Revelation, the Lord brings the church of Thyatira under judgment for its allowance of sexual perversion, namely fornication and adultery and goes further by highlighting Jezebel as the root of the problem.

As was shown in Chapter 1, the enemy is skilled in counterfeiting God's blue print. Please note, he cannot be good, and so he puts his own twist on things to ensure that he gets the glory. Just as heterosexual relations within the confines of marriage are pleasing, and a form of worship to God, the enemy has also designed sexual relations that bring glory to him – sexual perversion.

Takes Possessions.

Jezebel will seek to take from you that which has been bestowed upon you as a child of God: your gifting, your talent, your assignment and your destiny. Consider the example, the scenario with Naboth's vineyard.

> "And it came to pass after these things, that Naboth the Jezerelite had a vineyard which was in Jezreel, hard by the palace of Ahab king of Samaria. And Ahab spoke unto Naboth, saying, Give me thy vineyard, that I may have it for a garden of herbs: and I will give thee for a better vineyard than it; or, if it seems good to thee, I will give thee the worth of it in money. And Naboth said to Ahab, The Lord forbid it me, that I should give the inheritance of my fathers unto thee."
>
> -1 Kings 21:1-3 (KJV)

Ahab tried to purchase from Naboth a vineyard that he had been blessed with as an inheritance. While many people would have jumped at the opportunity to get a better vineyard or the monetary value for the vineyard, Naboth opted differently unlike Esau, who sold his birthright for a cup of stew (see Genesis 25:30-34). Naboth had great respect for God's command that every tribe keep the inheritance of their fathers and not transfer it (see Numbers 36:9).

Naboth's refusal of Ahab's offer made Ahab upset and even though Naboth explained the divine precepts that encouraged him in his decision, Ahab did not retreat. Instead, he brought the matter before Jezebel. Jezebel did for him what he knew was wrong and what he was reluctant to do himself.

> *"So she wrote letters in Ahab's name, and sealed them with his seal, and sent the letters unto the elders and to the nobles that were in the city, dwelling with Naboth. And she wrote in the letters saying, Proclaim a fast and set Naboth on high among the people: And set two men, sons of Belial, before him, to bear witness against him, saying, Thou didst blaspheme God and the King. And then carry him out, and stone him, that he may*

> *die...Then they sent to Jezebel, saying, Naboth is stoned, and is dead. And it came to pass, when Jezebel heard that Naboth was stoned, and was dead, that Jezebel said to Ahab, Arise, take possession of the vineyard of Naboth the Jezreelite, which he refused to give thee for money: for Naboth is not alive, but dead."*
>
> -1 Kings 21: 8-10, 14-15 (KJV)

The highlighted verses in 1 Kings 21, shows us that Jezebel devised a means to take Naboth's vineyard, but it also reveals to us that at that time, Jezebel also came into possession of Ahab's authority. The moment she wrote letters in his name and "sealed them with his seal," she had come into possession of the power to act on behalf of Ahab; to decree a thing like Ahab and to judge as Ahab did.

When Jezebel is in the house, it may appear that leadership is acting in a manner that is contrary to what they would do before their alliance with Jezebel; a manner that is contrary to the precepts and commands of God. Don't be surprised! It is because Jezebel has come into possession of authority; the harlot is acting on behalf of leadership and is willing to act in antithesis to the precepts of God to feed the desires and appetite of the tainted leader.

Drought and Desolation Come Upon the Land .

One of the most felt effects of Jezebel's presence was a divinely imposed drought. Several verses of Scripture enlighten us of the desolation that the people of Israel faced during her reign.

> "And Elijah the Tishbite, who was of the inhabitants of Gilead, said unto Ahab, As the Lord God of Israel liveth, before whom I stand, there shall not be dew nor rain these years, but according to my word."
> -1 Kings 17:1 (KJV)

> "And it came to pass after a while, that the brook [for Elijah's water] dried up, because there had been no rain in the land."
> -1 Kings 17:8 (KJV)

> "And she said, [to Elijah] 'As the Lord thy God liveth, I have not a cake, but an handful of meal in a barrel, and a little oil in a cruse: and, behold, I am gathering two sticks, that I may go in and dress it for me and my son, that we may eat it, and die.'"
> -1 Kings 17:12 (KJV)

> "And Ahab said unto Obadiah, 'Go into the land, unto all fountains of water, and unto all brooks: peradventure we may find grass to save the horses and mules alive, that we lose not all the beasts.'"
> -1 Kings 18:5 (KJV)

The preceding verses show that the land experienced starvation, people were hungry, and it would not be a stretch to say that livestock and agriculture experienced stunted growth and development. In the same way, when there is a harlot in the Church – when sexual immorality resides in the house of God – the Church will experience stunted growth and development and some will die spiritually.

There will be an un-assuaged hunger for spiritual food and the land (the Church) will be unable to produce enough to feed those who live on it. In other words, the congregants would be dissatisfied and always seeking for more. Even those who remain connected to God within such a congregation will experience the effects of the drought.

We know that Elijah was one of the few prophets remaining, yet we are told that the brook where he found his water was also dried up. From this account we come to an understanding that when sexual immorality is present in the church, both the faithful and unfaithful suffer.

But the Rain Came Back.

Amidst all the desolation in the land, somewhere in 2 Kings 18, came a new cry – *"an abundance of rain."* How is it that Jezebel (the harlot spirit) was still present but the land would be brought out of drought and desolation? How is it that the land would be transformed from cracked, broken and baked to fertility?

To answer these questions it is important to note the point at which Elijah prayed for rain in the land. His prayer for rain came after a showdown of the gods; after he had ordered the prophets of Ba-al to be killed. The sound of *"an abundance of rain"* came after the messengers of the god of the harlot had been eliminated from the land. The harlot was not yet removed; however, this was the genesis of a purging in Israel.

From this we learn two things – we learn that the purging of sexual immorality from a congregation is a process, but we also learn that the rain will come back only after the purging has commenced. If you lead a congregation that is suffering from the scourge of sexual immorality, be mindful that this scourge is not always something that leaves with immediacy.

Often times it is a time dependent and time consuming process. But also be hopeful, that amidst the process – as long as purging has commenced – God will send the rain back when he sees fit. He will do what is necessary to carry the Church into a place of spiritual restoration. Some things or some people may be lost in the process, but God will do what He said He will do and Christ proclaimed that the gates of hell shall not prevail against His Church.

ROTA - SEX IN THE CITY

CHAPTER FIVE

[DELILAH, THE PROFESSIONAL]

> *"And it came to pass afterward, that he loved a woman in the valley of Sorek, whose name was Delilah."*
>
> - Judges 16:4 (KJV)

Delilah is the professional harlot who brought Samson to his knees. The very meaning of Delilah's name reveals her purpose and intent in Samson's life. Delilah derives from a Hebrew word that means to slacken or to be feeble; to be oppressed; to bring low, be emptied, dry up; to fail; to be made weak and thin. She was a calculating and persistent woman whose actions were driven by the theme *"This is how I make my living."*

It seems that she had no aught against Samson, nor does it appear that she sought power in the ruling sphere. It was simply her job to weaken the defenses of Israel through her target of Samson. The spirit of harlotry as replicated in the life of Delilah attacks one's flesh. It knows and understands vulnerabilities and weaknesses. Its goal is to oppress, by presenting the spiritual challenge in the area of one's appetite, which in turn leads to mental, physical or emotional exhaustion and thus resulting in a lowered guard.

> *"And she said unto him, 'How canst thou say, I love thee, when thine heart is not with me? Thou hast mocked me these three times, and hast not told me wherein thy great strength lieth.' And it came to pass, when she pressed him daily with her words, and urged him, so that his soul was vexed unto death; that he told her all his heart..."*
>
> –Judges 16: 15-16 (KJV)

Delilah was the one who would be persistent in the use of her sexual wiles and in the application of deceitful care and concern, for a price. She was a professional. Her operations mirrored the precision of a hired assassin. She would not stop until she had attained the objectives that she would be paid for.

> *"And the lords of the Philistines came up unto her, and said unto her, 'Entice him, and see wherein his great strength lieth, and by what means we may prevail against him, that we may bind him to afflict him: and we will give thee every one of us eleven hundred pieces of silver.'"*
>
> – Judges 16:5 (KJV)

The interaction between Delilah, Samson and the Philistines is not dissimilar to the way in which the spirit of harlotry functions within the present-day Church. Just as Samson was supposed to serve the purpose of rescuer to the people of Israel, so too there are men and women of God within the Body of Christ who have been anointed and strategically ordained to set the captives free.

Just as the Philistines sought to hinder Samson in the fulfillment of his anointing, so too there is an enemy that seeks to devour the anointed men and women in the Body. Today, the enemy's tool is not Delilah, but a spirit of harlotry patterned after the actions of both the Philistines and Delilah.

The spirit of harlotry functions within the Church today, and recognizes those whom have been called to set the captives free, the contrary appetites, their weaknesses and vulnerabilities, as well as the challenge which they pose to the kingdom of darkness. In so doing, the spirit often works by presenting that which will fulfill these contrary appetites and it would not be amiss to say that often times, these contrary appetites are fed by that which constitutes sexual perversion.

With Samson, the symbol of his strength was his hair as it was representative of his covenant with God, but today the source of the strength of a strong man is found in the Spirit of God. It almost seems like the spirit of harlotry has an easier task than that of Delilah, because it doesn't have to identify particulars about the source of the strong man's strength; it simply needs to encourage the strong man to feed his appetite in a way that will grieve the Spirit of God. This will in turn lead to a disconnection from God, a result similar to the cutting of Samson's hair by Delilah.

Delilah works on the flesh; Samson is weak and tired, which is perfect prey for her. You lose your character in seconds, but it takes years to rebuild it. As his life progressed, he allowed himself to fall deeper and deeper into sin. He was allowing it to control him and turned his back on his promises to God. Though he was still accomplishing what God wanted him to do, inside his spirit was being weakened by the avenues he left open to the harlot spirit.

Delilah, his weakness, strikes at his lowest to result in his destruction. Things have not worked out the way he would have liked in his life, and enjoying Delilah allows him to forget the cares of his life. In the beginning, it was all a game to Samson, as he concocted various lies of how his strength could be diminished. He had been betrayed by his wife before and his people had betrayed him.

Every time Delilah attempted the lies he told her that would take his strength should have been red flags that this woman was nothing but trouble. For whatever reason though, he stayed with her and humored her. Whether his sexual desire for her was too great since he had sunk so deeply in sin or his love for her was real, we will never know.

We wonder, where were those who cared for Samson? Why were they not there to help him see the truth about these women especially Delilah? We do not know; the only thing we know is that his decision was his alone, and he chose poorly. He allowed a beautiful woman that made him frail to take all that he had left. How often has this been the case for men and women of God? It's almost as if believers are drawn to what's bad for them. The simplest attraction at times causes very rash responses and sadly detrimental repercussions.

ROTA - SEX IN THE CITY

CHAPTER SIX

[TAMAR, THE OPPORTUNIST]

I call Tamar the opportunistic harlot for the sole reason that her actions were not driven by need or principle, nor was she hired by anyone; the driving force behind her actions was the attainment of a desired goal – she wanted a male heir.

Interestingly, Tamar was not a harlot by trade. As a matter of fact, her circumstances suggest that she knew nothing of prostitution. But like a skilled entrepreneur, when the opportunity to get what she wanted presented itself, she wasted no time; she pounced on it even if it required her to be what she was not – a harlot. Tamar's story is told in Genesis Chapter 38. From the account, we know that she was married to Judah's eldest son Er and it appeared that she looked forward to bearing children – particularly a male heir. Yet, this was not to be so. Er was "wicked in the sight of the Lord" and God killed him.

According to the Levirate custom, Tamar would not be denied her desire to produce a male heir – one who would come into ownership of Er's possessions. One of Er's brothers would be required to stand in as a kinsman redeemer by marrying her and providing her with a male child. That male child would be considered Er's son, and would come into inheritance of Er's possessions.

> "And Judah said unto Onan, 'Go in unto thy brother's wife, and marry her, and raise up seed to thy brother.' And Onan knew that the seed should not be his; and it came to pass that he spilled it on the ground, lest that he should give seed to his brother. And this thing which he did displeased the Lord: wherefore he slew him also."
>
> - Genesis 38:8-9 (KJV)

Judah sent Onan, his second son to fulfill the role of kinsman redeemer. Still, this obligation was against Onan's wishes and so during his sexual relations with Tamar, he pulled out before ejaculation. This was displeasing to God, and the price paid was Onan's life. So there are two sons down, one to go! *"This woman is accursed!"* is what most likely plagued Judah's thought process. He knew that his last son Shelah was expected to step into the role of kinsman redeemer after Onan's death. But how could he allow such?

Each time he sent one of his sons to this woman they ended up dead. But Judah did not wish to appear dishonorable. So he promised Tamar that when Shelah was of age that he would send him in to fulfill his Levirate obligation of kinsman redeemer. The years went by and Shelah grew up. Still, Tamar remained unmarried and in waiting. But an opportunity came knocking and she kicked into high gear.

Judah's wife passed away (thus he was now eligible to fulfill the role of providing Tamar with an heir for Er). Tamar was informed that he would be going to Timnah for the shearing of his sheep, and she decided that this was the perfect opportunity to play the *"ho."* The account in Genesis 38 tells us that Tamar took off her mourning clothes and put on a veil to disguise her face and she positioned herself in a place where she knew that Judah had to pass to get to his destination. In the name of her aims, she deliberately became a prostitute.

> *"When Judah saw her, he thought her to be an harlot; because she had covered her face. And he turned unto her by the way, and said, 'Go to, I pray thee, let me come in unto thee;' (for*

> *he knew not that she was his daughter in law.) And she said, 'What wilt thou give me, that thou mayest come in unto me?' And he said, 'I will send thee a kid from the flock.' And she said, 'Wilt thou give me a pledge, till thou send it.' And he said, 'What pledge shall I give thee?' And she said, 'Thy signet, and thy bracelets, and thy staff that is in thine hand.' And he gave it her, and came in unto her, and she conceived by him."*
>
> - Genesis 38:15-18 (KJV)

Tamar's tactical setting is only the dawn of understanding the operations of this type of harlotry. Another key identifier is her ability to negotiate. Bargaining, deception and disguise are her characteristics. *"If you give me this, I will give you that" "If you do this for me, I will do that for you"* is the cry of this brand of harlotry. These negotiations are not without value, though.

This type of harlot will negotiate for that which will put its target in a position of compromise – a position that will force its target to plead for its salvation in the stead of its execution. When Judah propositioned Tamar, she knew that she had caught him unawares. The opportunity that Tamar presented to Judah was one marked by the limitations of time whereby he wanted her and he wanted her now.

This in turn caused Judah to act within the parameters of limited thought whereby he failed to consider that he did not have the means to pay her and so he found himself in a situation where he had to make a bargain with her to get what he wanted from her. Tamar was able to convince Judah to leave items of tremendous significance behind – his signet, his bracelets and his staff.

These items are spiritually significant and because of their worth, her life was saved where death should have been her portion. Judah gave away his name and his protection as he tied himself to someone who was not his wife.

The Bargain: The Items and Their Significance.

His Signet – A signet is symbolic of a signature. It was a tradition of the time whereby whoever wore it belonged to Judah. It represented his identity; it was his seal that bore his name. Once he gave it to Tamar, he was signing his oath; he was claiming her. Today when people get married, they exchange and wear rings to show this sense of belonging.

His Bracelets – These were cords and cords are ties that bind. When Judah gave Tamar his bracelets, he was binding her to him and to his house.

His Staff – The staff is a symbol of protection. The staff of a shepherd protected the sheep and kept them from straying. Judah's staff allowed Tamar to come under his protection. In the end it protected her from a harlot's fate. Now, allow me to parallel Judah and Tamar's scenario with the happenings in the present-day Church.

Just like Tamar, congregants make frequent use of deception and disguise to attain their desires and very often, like Tamar that which is targeted is Judah - the praise and the worship of the house. Thus, we see that sexual immorality within the Church will not only target leadership; it will also target the intimacy between God and His people; it will seek to eliminate the true presence of God in the church (the Lord inhabits the praises of His people).

There is another parallel which can be drawn when we examine the items bargained for. It relates to the treatment and the relationship of the harlot by those who are responsible for praise and worship in the Church. Often times just like Judah, those who are responsible for ushering the presence of God into the house (worship ministers) pamper sexual immorality.

Often times, they place their stamp on it, they go into covenant with it and it becomes holder to their identity. Others are bound to the scourge and many leaders will tell you that often times the sexual immorality comes under the protection of those responsible for praise and worship in the Church. Sexual immorality is hidden and kept under wraps; it is given a haven and a safe place of rest.

ILLUSION

The account of Tamar and Judah in Genesis 38 tells us that Judah gave Tamar the items, expecting them to be returned to him when he returned with a kid goat as payment for her services. However, when Judah sent his friend to pay Tamar, she was not at the place where Judah propositioned her.

> *"And Judah sent the kid by the hand of his friend the Adullamite, to receive his pledge from the woman's hand: but he found her not. Then he asked the men of that place, saying, Where is the harlot, that was openly by the way side? And they said, There was no harlot in this place. And he returned to Judah, and said, I cannot find her; and also the men of the place said, that there was no harlot in this place."*
>
> - Genesis 38: 20-22 (KJV)

His friend asked about the prostitute at the shrine, but the response was that there had never been a prostitute there; no one knew of a prostitute near the shrine. At this point, Judah's friend made a decision to retreat for fear of becoming the laughing stock of that village. He recognized that Judah had been deluded.

Sexual sin is never over; it has a way of coming back to haunt you, just as Tamar came back to haunt Judah. The consequences of sin, especially sexual sin is a burden people carry for years, even a lifetime. When sexual immorality is in the Church, praise and worship in the house will mimic the spirit of harlotry that targeted Judah. It will take on the personality of that which it has been joined to, that which it has slept with.

Tamar will hold Judah's bracelets. It will appear as an illusion. It will appear as though the Church has a worship team that ushers the true presence of God into the house, but just like Judah, one will come into the recognition that what one thought was there was actually not. For this reason, it is important to understand that one cannot determine the true presence of God in a house by excellent singing, grand displays of worship and well-orchestrated musical productions

Skills and talents achieve greatness, but the only way to truly tell whether the presence of God inhabits a particular house is by looking at the fruits manifested. If the Church is filled with love, joy and peace, then God's presence is there. If the people are patient, kind, and practice self-control, they are walking in the presence of God. If the people are faithful, then that church is in God's presence.

Equally, if you are in a place where the choir director is sleeping with the musician and unmarried ministers on the worship team are getting pregnant, no matter how great you deem the worship service, it is safe to say that there is a harlot in the house. It is clear that the spirit of harlotry reigns when people perform instead of worship. Worship is a lifestyle, so if there is no righteous living you have already distorted worship and invited the spirit of harlotry to roam free in your congregation.

ROTA - SEX IN THE CITY

CHAPTER SEVEN

[ONE NIGHT STAND]

When I speak of a one night stand here, it does not necessarily refer to one night of sex with a stranger or someone who you don't know too well. Rather, I am referring to short term pleasure; something that appeases the flesh leaving you only wanting more. Sin is the enemy's lure so he uses fornication, masturbation, pornography, homosexuality, etc. He will employ every possible deviation to God's provision.

We have looked at three main characters, namely Samson, David and Judah, and find one thing in common with these men. Each of these men made life changing decision for a moment of pleasure. Many times, lives are destroyed not only physically but also spiritually, mentally, socially and emotionally, because someone wanted temporary gratification.

We also see that each of these men had issues within themselves that were not dealt with. Samson was the wounded warrior, David the covetous King and Judah the restless father. It's important to note that you cannot and must not make a destiny decision dependent on what you see in the present but it must be based on God's purpose for your life. I believe the problem lies in the appetite we hold and how to facilitate the appetite.

As a man you need to know who you are and what it is you are carrying (the seed). There are those with a big sexual appetite, but they are not married and others who may be married, but are not having their appetite adequately satisfied at home. The devil wants us to facilitate the appetite in an ungodly way; he proposes a *"quick fix"*.

Let's look at another Biblical personality – Esau. He was working for his father, but was hungry. There are many believers who are loved by God and in ministry but are hungry. Satisfying the spiritual and ignoring the physical can cause problems. So he came home one day famished and smelling an irresistible stew being cooked by his brother. Upon requesting some, he was manipulated into selling his birthright to quell his hunger. Once again a huge decision, wrecking the future of the man, is made for a brief indulgence.

When you become starved, the appetite becomes intense and leaves you willing to do anything to satisfy the desire you bear. He was so desperate that he dropped his guard, lowering his standard. Many times when people get caught up in sexual immorality it is with someone below their level; it is often, for the singles, with people they may never see themselves marrying or for the married, with people who cannot measure up to their spouses.

The harlot spirit knows how to exchange; you don't hook up with a harlot and come back empty-handed. The devil knows what we like and how we like it and he prepares what we will fall for and presents it just when we feel that is exactly what we need. The spirit has no problem with your worship and witness, but knows your weakness. He offers what you think you can't live without.

The principality of immorality have held the Church in bondage for too long and now God wants to free us and raise up some men who will confront the system. To step into that dimension of ministry you will need a prayer life, a consistent relationship with God, a kingly anointing like David, a worshipper's mentality like Judah, a warrior spirit like Samson. You will need a conscious, deliberate commitment to develop your character into that realm. There are some folks in bondage that only you can set free. Recognize your purpose and destiny so no matter who or what comes, you will stand.

Israel was depending on Samson. To set a generation free, you must follow God's instructions. We are all called to prominence, but we have character flaws and what is needed is righteousness. I have to be able to submit and let God deal with the issues in my life. Samson started to descend the ladder and made a destiny decision based on his present state – big mistake. When he fell, he lost his strength, his integrity, his position and his sight.

How many of us can safely say we will never succumb to the temptations the devil flaunts. We must be careful of what we crave because at the tiny moment of peak desire, the unguarded moment, we can abolish our purpose, mission and goals in life.

CHAPTER EIGHT

[MARRIED TO A STRIPPER]

No, I am not speaking of a lady who dances and takes off her clothes for a living; I am referring to the one and only Jesus Christ; the only One who can rid you of all sexual sin and urges associated with them. God is committed to us and thus obligated to deal with every issue in our lives. No matter what the struggle is, the Stripper can take it away.

Some of us feel unworthy because of the spirits and strongholds we have invited into our lives and we see that there are physical, mental and spiritual implications to sexual immorality. Sexual immorality opens the doors not only for spirits, but also for curses to be applied to our lives. When God is covering you, your duty is to walk upright and the enemy cannot touch you.

The enemy changes his strategies and his approach because he studies you and learns you. If you know the protection that is over you and what is going on in the spirit realm on your behalf, you will behave differently. When we step out in sin, we also step away from the covering of Christ into dangerous territory, giving the enemy free reign in our lives.

We must all keep check on our association. Most of the stuff we engage in is influenced by those people and things we associate with. If you want to stay holy there are some places you cannot go and some folks you cannot hang out with. What fellowship can light have with darkness? Make a destiny decision in choosing where you go, who you go with and what you do there. Some things you allow into your spirit take power and rights to make some impact on your life.

If you cannot identify the plan, plot and predicament of the devil, you will be in trouble. To the singles: stop being desperate for a relationship and wait on God. To the spouses: learn to be content with the person YOU chose to marry and trust God to improve the marriage. Be wise and discerning. Do not give up the prize until he takes you to the altar. Your mind needs to be transformed by the Word of God. Some come to Christ, so their spirit is saved, but the mind needs renewal.

When God is displeased, judgment comes to eradicate sin. It must be cut from the head not covered up. When these things are not dealt with, there is always a fluctuating relationship with God. God wants to strip us from the sexual issues we face as well as the spirits behind them. The gift of salvation means we are saved from the universal penalty of eternal death and now have eternal life.

On the other hand, if a believer is living in sin or being controlled by a sinful desire, he/she cannot be said to be saved and hence separate from the promises and headship of Christ. When spirits and curses enter our lives, we develop all manner of ungodly thoughts, attitudes and behaviors which all need to be stripped by the only person who can, Jesus. Let's look at how we can avoid this dilemma.

CHAPTER NINE

[CONTROLLING YOUR APPETITE]

> *"Let no man say when he is tempted, I am tempted of God: for God cannot be tempted with evil, neither tempteth he any man: But every man is tempted when he is drawn away of his own lust and enticed."*
>
> - James 1:13-14 (KJV)

You have read about the different types of harlot spirits that are waiting to entrap men and women of the Holy City. Now, allow me to help you understand the appetites the men and women have that can be a feeding ground for these spirits.

In dealing with sexual immorality from a male and female perspective, you find out some interesting things about the differences in how we think and can see how the spirits draw each gender based on such. We will be biblical and first look at these things from a male perspective.

THE MALE:

You have read about Samson the fallen warrior, David the humbled king and Judah the lost worshipper. We will continue to use these men as examples to illustrate the uncontrollable male appetite. Men are moved and motivated by what they see. They are also highly intrigued by what is under the surface of what they see — the things that are hidden.

As strange as it may seem to women, men deeply desire what they cannot see or thirst to get things that they cannot get. That is why males are more likely to be hunters. A hunter pursues his prey as a conquest and is more excited about the chase than he is about the actual catch. Whether he realizes it or not, every man is built with the ability and desire to conquer.

God created men that way, so He knows that men are driven by the things that they want—by their appetites. Before we go any further, I want to make sure that you understand what I mean by the word appetite. The Oxford American Dictionary defines the word appetite as a natural desire to satisfy a bodily need, especially for food. The word comes from the old French word apetit (modern appétit) and from the Latin appetites which both mean to have a desire for.

This is good on one hand – it allows men to achieve goals with a single-mindedness that is not found in women. It also allows man to detach himself from the emotional side of the battle (how many lives will be lost?) to look at the overall good of winning the battle (we will surpass).

It is bad on the other hand, because men are frequently encouraged by the world today to let their appetites roam wild, and an appetite that is not under control is like an out-of-control truck that can cause very tragic accidents. I will show you how to control your appetite, so it can be used for the honor and glory of God.

When the Bible talks about Samson, it says he went down to Timnah and saw a woman. After seeing her, he told his mother and father get her for him, because she pleased him well. Samson was contented with what he saw (she looks good) and was satisfied with what he tasted (she pleases me well). That's appetite!!!

King David, the Bible says, was on his veranda and he saw Bathsheba taking a bath. He looked, he lusted and he lay. David was contented with what he saw. David was so contented with what he saw that he sent for her and slept with her to mollify his appetite. That's appetite!!!

Judah saw Tamar dressed as a harlot on the side of the road. She could give him what he wanted at the moment, so he was willing to give her anything as payment for it. That's appetite!!!

You are the one who has to deal with the errors in your life. It begins with whom you are hanging around or in other words, who you are dating; be wise in your dating. If you are single and trying to control your appetite, but you say, "I need a wife, now, to help me!" it will not help; your heart will yearn. Instead, trust God to provide as He has done for countless people before you.

> *"Wait on the Lord; be of good courage, and he shall strengthen then hear; wait, I say, on the Lord."*
>
> - Psalms 27:14 (KJV)

Waiting on God is never in vain. You do not want to choose a marriage partner in haste only to find out you have chosen someone below your standard. Samson ended up heart broken, weak, lonely, blind and then dead. All of it was gone in one second because he shared his secret with the wrong woman. It took him years of captivity in order to build it back up. Simple misjudgments of people can cost us our lives.

Having an appetite is not wrong because we are appetite driven. God has placed this appetite in us to be used for good. The good appetites include an appetite for prayer, for worship, for His presence, for His Word, etc. As men we also have other appetites that can be good or bad depending on how we control them such as sex, money and power.

When a man is unable to control his appetites, he endangers himself and those around him. It is important to learn how to put your appetites and every other thing in your life under subjection. These are the top three areas of the appetite for men to subject to God's will. If these areas are not controlled, it can cause great disaster for the man.

Having an appetite for sex is simply a craving for it. It is the way that you fulfill your appetites that can become sinful. The truth remains that you can act on your appetite in bad ways and still not be fulfilled. If you are not married or are not satisfied with what you are getting at home and you make the decision to step outside of God's will in order to fulfill your desire for sex, then your appetite has the power to ruin your life.

> "And when he had fasted forty days and forty nights, he was afterward hungered. And when the tempter came to him, he said, 'If thou be the Son of God, command that these stones be made bread.' But he answered and said, 'It is written, Man shall not live by bread alone, but by every word that proceedeth out of the mouth of God.'"
>
> - Matthew 4:2-4 (KJV)

When Jesus was tempted in the wilderness, He was hungry since He had not eaten for forty days. His appetite was immense; but when the devil came to Him and tempted Him by telling Him to turn stones into bread, Jesus did not give in to the temptation. The devil knew who Jesus was, but he asked for proof. Jesus knew who He was and refused.

As long as you know who you are, you will not have to prove your identity to others. If you are not sure about your identity in Christ, you will find yourself doing things you have no right doing just to feel a particular way or to prove to people your identity. He knows where your weakness is: He did not come to Jesus and ask him to turn the stones into a table. He always brings what you want the most and comes at the time when you are the weakest and most vulnerable.

The devil took a legitimate appetite for food, mixed with desire and passion, and twisted it hoping it would become lust. If you understand where I am heading with this, you would realize that lust is a defiant passion gone wild. You have believers in church who have a legitimate passion and desire, but because it has not been brought under the Lordship of Jesus Christ, it eventually turns into lust.

> *"But every man is tempted, when he is drawn away of his own lust and enticed. Then when lust hath conceived, it bringeth forth din: and sin, when it is finished, bringeth forth death."*
>
> - James 21:14-15 (KJV)

I am absolutely certain that none of us would want to be in a church that is filled with lustful leaders. We all have a longing within us for the presence of God. The church should be filled with believers who have a passion for the things that will bring glory to God, such as worship and soul-winning.

God takes your appetites, passions, and desires, and He begins to speak the mind of Christ into them. Jesus could have turned those stones into bread because He had the power to do it, but He refused because His desire to please His heavenly Father was greater than His appetite for food. The enemy does the very same thing when it comes to our appetite for sex.

Driven by our hunger, our appetite is fuelled with desires and passions. There are opportunities all around us for them to be satisfied, but God wants us to satisfy them His way. Allow me to paint this scenario to you: you are a pastor or a leader in the church with folks all around you. You are in a position of authority and a person of influence and the enemy knows you are hungry.

If your appetite is not under control, great havoc and destruction can come. Many fall into this snare of the enemy, but as we continue we will see how Jesus dealt with His appetite and if Jesus did it, so can we. The same way God can shape your desires into passions that are pleasing to him, the devil is able to take our sexual desires and shape them into something perverted.

Just as the devil would not have had to tell Jesus how to turn stones into bread, he does not have to tell us how to fulfill our lusts. God has provided a place of fulfillment for every desire that we have, including sex. He created marriage between a man and a woman for the purpose of procreation and satisfying our sexual appetites.

When sex is in my thoughts and on my mind, it means that I am hungry: my appetite has been aroused and my desire is at its peak for my wife. She then fulfills that appetite for me in a way that is pleasing to God, within the context of our marital relationship.

> *"Marriage is honorable in all, and the bed undefiled: but whoremongers and adulterers God will judge."*
>
> - Hebrews 13:4 (KJV)

If you are having sex within the confines of the covenant of marriage, God honors and blesses that covenant. Any method I look for that will fulfill or satisfy my appetite for sex outside this God given arena is illegal and considered fornication or adultery. Many people fall into this trap and I call it a trap because it is systematically plotted out by the enemy in order to trap us into sin.

Remember that there is a hit on your life and the devil is looking for a way to take you down. He will use every means available to him for that purpose and the wages of sin is death so the devil gets the victory any time he can get a believer to die in sin. God has given us provisions to satisfy our appetites on every level.

He has given us food to satisfy physical hunger, the Bible to satisfy our hunger for His Word, the ability to work to satisfy our desire for money, and he has given us marriage to fulfill our desire for sex. He never intends for our sexual appetites to be fulfilled through masturbation, fornication, adultery and homosexuality.

These are ungodly, illegal ways that the devil uses, tempting us to satisfy that urge now, in a way that is destructive. Let's pause here to examine and compare the appetites of Esau and Joseph and how they managed them.

ESAU

Esau depicts the behavior of a believer who is working in ministry, but is not able to control his appetite. Esau was willing to give away his inheritance just for the satisfaction of a onetime selfish desire. Many in ministry who have become corrupted by sexual immorality live under the same premise: they do not care about the end results of their actions they just want what they want, now!

> *"And the boys grew: and Esau was a cunning hunter, a man of the field; and Jacob was a plain man, dwelling in tents. And Isaac loved Esau, because he did eat of his venison: but Rebekah loved Jacob. And Jacob sod pottage: and Esau came*

> *from the field and he was faint: And Esau said to Jacob, Feed me, I pray thee, with that same red pottage; for I am faint: therefore was his name called Edom. And Jacob said, 'Sell me this day thy birthright.' And Esau said, Behold, I am at the point to die: and what profit shall this birthright do to me?' And Jacob said swear to me this day; and he sware unto him: and he sold his birthright unto Jacob. Then Jacob gave Esau bread and pottage of lentils; and he did eat and drink, and rose up, and went his way: thus Esau despised his birthright."*
>
> - Genesis 25:27-34 (KJV)

As the firstborn, Esau was entitled to a double portion of his father's estate. He would get 2/3 of the inheritance while Jacob only received 1/3. In addition, Esau would be carrying on the line of his father and because this lineage was the ancestry of Jesus, Esau was the one who should have been listed in Jesus' genealogy.

He would have been given a double blessing. However, Esau did not care about these things at the moment of his hunger. He sold all of this off for one bowl of stew to satisfy his appetite. I pause here to ask, what is the value of the anointing in your life? Or what value do you place on your life and position? This can encompass your marriage, your ministry, or you as a person.

If you don't know what you have or what you are carrying, abuse is inevitable because you only cherish what you understand and place a high value on. The Bible says that Esau was loved by his father and did what the father liked. There was no evidence of sustenance manifesting in Esau's life. Often times we see this in churches today where you have folks serving God for years, but not manifesting any evidence of the kingdom in their life.

This can be frustrating for a believer, especially when you know you are loved by the Father and doing what the Father likes. You can be serving in ministry with your whole heart but still be hungry. The blessings of God are not automatic, but must be appropriated by faith. For every promise and every prophecy in the Word of God and that was spoken over your life, there is a faith process to bring it to pass.

When we look at this to apply it to today, Esau is a type of the believer in ministry doing what the Father (God) likes; he is working in the field and in the world, building up an appetite. Even though he is working in ministry, he has an appetite that is too great. In fact, it seems like the ministry or the work he is doing is not satisfying him in this area of his life.

Like many of us in Christendom hungrily doing ministry, we do not know how to control our appetite. We want more power, more money, and more of our appetite filled. We will sell our birthright for a meal that is nowhere near the cost we pay. When Esau is coming out of the field hungry and meets his brother, he asks him for assistance. Now there are several things wrong with this scenario.

Firstly, Esau acts as if he is going to die. Now, if you are working in the field, do not stay out there until your appetite is so strong you feel like you are going to die. Had Esau come in at the first nudge of his hunger, he could have prepared his own meal, he would not have died from it, but to Esau, it felt like he was going to die; he had worked in the field too long without a break.

Secondly, do not make your situation more desperate than its reality. Esau was not going to die; he could have easily gone home and made something else to eat. But his hunger was controlling his actions, and he wanted what he could get, immediately. He made his situation worse than it was, convinced himself that he was going to die, and told himself the only way out was to accept Jacob's offer.

Now, Jacob, whose name means, "to deceive" or literally "leg puller" was waiting there with food. Take note of this: Esau is asking assistance from somebody who does not work in the field and whose name means deception. Be careful whom you trust and associate with. When you associate with those outside the church, hold them at arm's length. When you go to them and ask favors of them, you may end up giving more than you are getting.

The harlot spirit works through Jacob's trickery. He responds, "Yes, I will help you, but it will cost you something." The enemy will not allow you to eat from his table without having it cost you something. It may cost you your ministry, your marriage, your integrity, or your entire character. These things will go in a second even though it takes years to build or regain them.

After giving in to temptation to satisfy your hunger, people's perception of you is tainted and when this occurs, it takes years to rebuild it if you ever manage to rebuild it. Although God has a way of turning things around for those who remain in Him, it may or may not return you to the position you held before you failed. Are you desperate? The enemy feeds on your desperation and encourages your lusts so that you will sin:

> "But every man is tempted when he is drawn away of his own lust and enticed. Then when lust hath conceived, it bringeth forth sin: and sin, when it is finished, bringeth forth death."
>
> - James 1:14 & 15 (KJV)

Here we see again the Harlot spirit in a bargain: "You give me this, and I give you that!" You are tempted by your own desires, not by God. The enemy is anticipating your hunger because he studies you so well and will not tempt you in an area where there is no need. He tempts you by offering you what you desire without you having to do the things that please God. In this context, your desires become lusts, which cause you to sin and eventually lead to death.

You need to understand that the devil does not mind you going to church, speaking in tongues, giving out biblical tracts, shouting, testifying or even preaching because he knows that eventually you will come home, and you will be hungry. He is banking on the fact that one day you will be vulnerable and susceptible enough for him to present his temptation.

As Bishop Noel Jones preached in his message *"Double Anointing,"* the Holy Ghost will have to sit upon you in that moment. If he does not, you will lose your church, your marriage, your mind and your ministry. Without the presence of God in your life at the moment of temptation, you will lose everything.

Familiar spirits know your areas of weakness. A familiar spirit is an unclean spirit that was assigned to you early in your life. It has had time to study you, and knows almost everything about you. It knows where you are vulnerable, and where you are strong. Its mission is to stop you from stepping out into your destiny by reminding you of all the things that you do not have and want. It is basically familiar with every aspect of your life and therefore can work through those who are close to you, including family members.

> "Lest there be any fornicator, or profane person, as Esau, who for one morsel of meat sold his birthright. For ye know how that afterward, when he would have inherited the blessing, he was rejected: for he found no place of repentance though he sought it carefully with tears."
>
> - Hebrews 12:16 & 17 (KJV)

I want you to consider something now: What is the value that you place on your life - your marriage, your ministry and yourself as a person? Do you know what your life is worth? Are you willing to ruin it in the pursuit of pleasure? If you do not understand the anointing that God has placed within you, then you will inevitably misuse it and abuse it. You only value and cherish those things that you know are worth something.

There is no evidence of growth manifesting in Esau's life. Oftentimes, we see this in churches today. This can be frustrating for us as believers; it sometimes seems like the work we are doing is in vain. If we are in ministry, we do not feel as though we should be hungry because we expect to see the fruit of our labors.

Unfortunately, there are times in the ministry when we do not get to see the extent of that fruit. You pray, and you might not think your prayers are being answered but you must hold strong to your faith. Faith doesn't have a timeline so after having faith for a certain period of time are you allowed to give up. No! You must keep the faith until Christ chooses to intervene.

> *"Who then is Paul, and who is Apollos, but ministers by whom ye believed, even as the Lord gave to every man? I have planted, Apollos watered; but God gave the increase. So then neither is he that planteth any thing, neither he that watereth; but God that giveth the increase. Now he that planteth and he that watereth are one: and every man shall receive his own reward according to his own labour. For we are labourers together with God: ye are God's husbandry, ye are God's building."*
>
> -1 Corinthians 3:5-9 (KJV)

When the person does not hold strong, he looks around and wants more than what is given at the time. The minister begins to feel as though neither the work of the ministry nor anything else in his life can fulfill the desire that he has. Get control of that appetite! If you are hungry in the ministry and do not know how to control that desire, it will control you.

Have you ever walked where food is being prepared? Sometimes just the scent of it will make you hungry even if you were not hungry before. Once you get that smell in your nose, your mouth begins to water, and you can almost taste it. It smells so good that you want to have it. Before you know it, you have convinced yourself that you have to have it.

The enemy will not allow you to eat from his table for free. He will present you with what you need or want, and it will look good, it will smell wonderful, it will sound perfect. You will even taste it, without even putting it in your mouth. The longer you examine it, the more you will want it; but it will cost you more than you realize at the time. You may never get some of those precious things back in your lifetime.

In analyzing the appetite for sex, men are generally not crazed for every woman they come across unless they have allowed the depths of sexual immorality to have complete control over them and diminish them to that. Conversely, even the most devout and faithful Christian who is following God's Word may have one particular woman that he is weak about. It is not everything but it's that one thing.

The harlot spirit knows one day you will come from the field hungry because your human side is not satisfied even though your divine side is. This is why Paul spoke about having moderation and the struggle between the spirit and the flesh.

> *"For we know that the law is spiritual: but I am carnal, sold under sin. For that which I do I allow not: for what I would, that do I not; but what I hate, that do I. If then I do that which I would not, I consent unto the law that it is good. Now then it is no more I that do it, but sin that dwelleth in me. For I know that in me (that is, in my flesh,) dwelleth no good thing: for to will is present with me; but how to perform that which is good I find not. For the good that I would I do not: but the evil which I would not, that I do. Now if I do that I would not, it is no more I that do it, but*

> *sin that dwelleth in me. I find then a law, that, when I would do good, evil is present with me. For I delight in the law of God after the inward man: But I see another law in my members, warring against the law of my mind, and bringing me into captivity to the law of sin which is in my members. O wretched man that I am! who shall deliver me from the body of this death? I thank God through Jesus Christ our Lord. So then with the mind I myself serve the law of God; but with the flesh the law of sin."*
>
> - Romans 7:14-25 (KJV)

Like Esau, the thought of food to eat is already in your mind while you were in the field working. Esau already knew what he wanted because he kept a picture of it in his mind while he was working. He let his imagination, taste it before he got home from the field. He saw it in his mind, he ate it in his mind, and he told himself that he needed it in his mind.

Now, he was imagining that it belonged to him, that it was already waiting for him. Then when he walked into the camp, there it was. When we allow our imagination to run free and we begin thinking about things that are not ours – things we should not have, it fills our minds and fuels our appetite.

This can be a powerful driving force behind our passion and desire that makes it more difficult to control.

Stop thoughts before they rage! It is said that half of the battle is won in your mind so protect and purify your thoughts carefully. Whenever you enter a difficult situation, you are always given a choice. You must decide: should I sell out or should I turn down this offer? Many who have accepted the offer, regret it afterward. We did not know how to control our appetites and we suffered for it.

Once we have been caught in that trap, we work hard to warn others: Do not follow this way. The harlot spirit is present in Esau's story, but it does not come through a woman; it comes through a man—Jacob—Esau's own twin brother. If you are a man, do not think that you only need to worry about women. There are men around who can tempt you in other ways or even arrange for your fall. Jacob's brother had a lifetime of living with Esau to study him, so he knew what to tempt him with.

If you have a sexual appetite that is out of control, you may try to rationalize it by telling yourself, "I don't go crazy for every woman I see. It is not a problem for me. I do not have to worry about this temptation. My appetite is normal." But then there is this one woman who you just cannot keep out of your mind, and she is not your wife. It's not everything; it's this one nagging desire that is distracting you.

The familiar spirit, that is attached to you knows that one day you will come home from ministering and your human side will be hungry for that one thing that you desire, even though you are completely fulfilled spiritually. That is why Paul spoke about having a balance in the areas of body, soul and spirit.

> *"And we beseech you, brethren, to know them which labour among you, and are over you in the Lord, and admonish you; And to esteem them very highly in love for their work's sake. And be at peace among yourselves. Now we exhort you, brethren, warn them that are unruly, comfort the feebleminded, support the weak, be patient toward all men. See that none render evil for evil unto any man; but ever follow that which is good, both among yourselves, and to all men. Rejoice evermore. Pray*

> *without ceasing. In everything give thanks: for this is the will of God in Christ Jesus concerning you. Quench not the Spirit. Despise not prophesying. Prove all things; hold fast that which is good. Abstain from all appearance of evil."*
>
> *- 1 Thessalonians 5:12-22 (KJV)*

If you are neglecting any of those areas, it makes it easier for the devil to tempt you. All the things that you desire are like that stew Esau sold out for. Maybe it is not food; it is the money for the electricity bill or for rent. You do not have an inheritance from your parents to sell, but you do have your body. Are you willing to risk your anointing by selling your body to get money for a bill? That familiar spirit tells you that it is just this one time, but once it happens you have lost something precious that you may not be able to get back.

You see, Jacob realized something that Esau did not. Esau saw his birthright as something that he would get in the distant future that was useless at the time, but Jacob knew that his father did not have long to live on earth and would be passing that blessing on sooner than Esau knew.

The devil knows that you are following the Word of God for a purpose – to save your soul. Those things promised to you, are almost within reach so if he can distract you from your goals, if he can get in front of you and block your view of what God is trying to do for you, then he can get you to sell out your blessings and your destiny.

He knows that God is able and willing to provide all of your needs, but if he can get you to temporarily forget that, he can get you to stumble and fall. Right now, you and I have a choice to make. We are free to decide whether we will sell out for the things that we desire or wait on God to provide for us in every area.

JOSEPH

> "But he [Joseph] refused and said unto his master's wife, Behold, my master wotteth not what is with me in the house, and he hath committed all that he hath to my hand; There is none greater in this house than I' neither hat he held back anything from me but thee because thou art his wife: how then can I do this great wickedness and sin against God?"
>
> - Genesis 39:8 & 9 (KJV)

Joseph was a young man favored by God and man. Potiphar's slave, but eventually Potiphar gave him a position of influence in his house, but this made Joseph a point of focus to Potiphar's wife. Now, Joseph had appetites just like Potiphar's wife did. However, Joseph handled his appetite differently from the way that Mrs. Potiphar handled hers. Nothing exempted Joseph from the normal urges of an unmarried young man.

Brother Joseph reminded himself that although he was not married, Potiphar's wife was – off course. He treated her the way that a brother in the Holy City should treat a sister, and kept her at a distance as best he could. He knew that she was interested in him and was pursuing him. So, he only did business with her when he had to. During this period, many slaves would have jumped at the opportunity that was presented to Joseph.

Unlike the wife of Potiphar who had everything she needed and desired; Joseph was a slave. He was not free to pursue the life that he wanted. He had no money and no way of obtaining it for himself, he had no woman and could not have married unless a wife was given to him, and he had no power except what he was entrusted with and what could be taken away in an instant even if he did well with it.

Joseph did not have the physical comforts that Potiphar's wife took for granted, but he did have something within him that she did not. Our brother had made a decision to live his life based on moral principles given to him by God, not on his own passions and wisdom. Because of that decision, he could not give Potiphar's wife what she wanted from him.

His response to her clearly indicated that a sexual relationship with her would be a sin against his God, and he could not do that. He did not question or debate his decision. He simply said, "No, I cannot do this." Joseph was a common man in an uncommon place. His story illustrates how any believer can control his/her appetite in spite of what has been offered, where they are, and the circumstances surrounding them.

Both Esau and Joseph had appetites and were presented with avenues to have these appetites gratified. Nevertheless, Esau set himself up and gave in to the sinful option while Joseph chose the better way, the path that would honor God. Maintaining your character and protecting your gifts are more valuable than any short term pleasure to fill a temporary appetite.

How did Jesus Control His appetite?

Jesus was faced with a situation that was similar to Esau's. He had gone forty days without food, and his human body was hungry. Like Jacob's quick solution to Esau's hunger problem—a bowl of lentil stew in exchange for his birthright—the devil offered Jesus a quick solution. He told Him to turn the stones into bread, and prove that He was the Son of God. Jesus himself said:

> *"Man shall not live by bread alone, but by every word that proceedeth out of the mouth of God"*
>
> - Matthew 4:4 (KJV)

What he meant when he said "by bread alone" is that bread is for eating, and it satisfies the flesh, but bread cannot satisfy the spirit. Jesus was reminding us that it takes more than feeding the physical appetite to sustain a whole person. Remember, you are not just your body. You are made up of body, soul and spirit. In Matthew 4, the word that is translated as "word" is rhema—which is a Greek word that means utterance. It is what you have received when you feel as though the words of the Bible were written directly for you.

The rhema or Word of God—the revelation from him—is food for your spirit and is no less important than bread is for the body. The only way to control your physical appetites for sex, food and any other desires is to feed and strengthen your spirit. If you have developed your spiritual side, when the fleshly desire arises, you can align it to what God wants for your life.

You strengthen your spirit through prayer, fasting and study of the Word. In doing this, you are enabling your spirit to control your physical appetites.

> *"And God said, Let us make man in our image, after our likeness: and let them have dominion over the fish of the sea, and over the fowl of the air, and over the cattle, and over all the earth, and over every creeping thing that creepeth upon the earth. So God created man in his own image, in the image of God created he him; male and female created he them."*
>
> *- Genesis 1:26-27(KJV)*

We are created in the image of God. When Jesus came, He showed us that it is possible for us to control our appetites. We need to be sure to hold them with tight reins.

> *"What is man, that thou art mindful of him? and the son of man, that thou visitest him? For thou hast made him a little lower than the angels, and hast crowned him with glory and honour. Thou madest him to have dominion over the works of thy hands; thou hast put all things under his feet:"*
>
> *- Psalms 8:4-6 (KJV)*

If we were created in His image, to be like Him on the earth, then we have the same power and authority that Jesus had to speak His Word and take control of a situation or temptations. Even though Jesus was the Son of God, He lived in a human body just like ours. He controlled the appetites that any human body has and thus we too can control our physical appetites, no matter how we are tempted. Keep His Word in your heart and mind and use it to fend off the temptation darts of the devil.

Fasting is a very important aspect of controlling the sexual appetite. Denying your flesh food helps to discipline it, and disciplined flesh is better able to resist temptation than undisciplined flesh. Fasting does not mean that you will not be tempted, but it does mean that you will be able to make better decisions when you are tempted because you will be used to not getting what you want immediately.

It lets the flesh know that you want to please God more than you want to please your body. It's a form of putting flesh under the subjection of the Spirit. Disciplining your flesh is essential to receiving and remaining in deliverance. Deliverance includes repenting of your sins and having demonic spirits cast out of you. If you do not allow God's spirit within you to take over your life, you face the danger of the spirits coming back seven times worse than they were before.

> *"When the unclean spirit is gone out of a man, he walketh through dry places, seeking rest, and findeth none. Then he saith, I will return into my house from whence I came out; and when he is come, he findeth it empty, swept, and garnished. Then goeth he, and taketh with himself seven other spirits more wicked than himself, and they enter in and dwell there: and the last state of that man is worse than the first."*
>
> - Matthew 12:43-45 (KJV)

When you turn to God, you need to be sure you have allowed the Holy Spirit to work within you. Without the guidance of the Holy Spirit, you are lost and will return to sin because the spirits that were inside you before will come back and bring their friends. If your flesh is disciplined by the Holy Spirit, you are better able to listen to God's revelation, and He is better able to order your steps.

> *"This I say then, Walk in the Spirit, and ye shall not fulfill the lust of the flesh. For the flesh lusteth against the Spirit, and the Spirit against the flesh: and these are contrary the one to the other: so that ye cannot do the things that ye would. But if ye be led of the Spirit, ye are not under the law. Now the works of the flesh are manifest, which are these; adultery, fornication, uncleanness, lasciviousness, Idolatry, witchcraft, hatred,*

> *variance, emulations, wrath, strife, seditions, heresies, envyings, murders, drunkenness, revellings, and such like: of the which I tell you before, as I have also told you in time past, that they which do such things shall not inherit the kingdom of God. But the fruit of the Spirit is love, joy, peace, longsuffering, gentleness, goodness, faith, Meekness, temperance: against such there is no law. And they that are Christ's have crucified the flesh with the affections and lusts. If we live in the Spirit, let us also walk in the Spirit. Let us not be desirous of vainglory, provoking one another, envying one another.*
>
> - Galatians 5:16-26 (KJV)

You will know a man by his fruit. If you are associating with people who are not bearing good fruit, you need to change your friends. The fruits of the spirit show us a person's true nature. Paul also says that there is no good thing in the flesh; you cannot trust it to make decisions that will affect your life; you cannot trust your emotions or your own mind either.

You must learn to trust God to guide your decisions. By learning to fill your spirit with the Word of God, and learning to trust in God's wisdom, we can begin to live lives that are more pleasing in His sight. Living your life by these principles keeps you from ruining your life with poor choices.

THE FEMALE

Like men, women have appetites that need to be placed under control as well. However, women are more likely than men to be moved by their emotions. Women are created to be emotional beings. When I say emotional, I mean that she is easily excited and is open with her feelings in a way that men usually are not. It is hard for a woman to hide her emotions.

Because she is responsible for the keeping of the home and she often has to work outside the home, she may sometimes appear to be many different things to many different people. Her life is like an orange. You may have one orange, but when you peel it you notice that it has several different segments. She compartmentalizes her life into many different segments, including work, home, and ministry, but she is still one person.

There are six to seven segments in an orange, and these parts represent the different compartments of a woman's life. Just like the orange with seeds, the woman holds the seed of God that was placed within her from the foundation of the world. Even though a woman may be crushed, hurt, bruised, or battered, God can reach down into her defeated state of life and pull out the seed and replant her on her path.

When replanted by God, she will flourish as she did before. As a woman, if you get down, get back into the Word of God and He will replant you on the right track. Her appetites are similar to men's appetites, but her motivations are different because all of her appetites are driven by an overwhelming need for security in three areas: attention and protection; money or provision; and power or management.

Fulfillment in all of these areas helps to make a woman feel secure. If she does not have a man, a woman will begin to feel lonesome and unprotected. She will not often seek money for its own sake, but she is driven to take care of her family and will seek money for that reason. If a woman is not allowed to manage her household, she can be made to feel useless and will seek other ways to manage things.

> *"And it came to pass after these things, that his master's [Potiphar's] wife cast her eyes upon Joseph: and she said, Lie with me."*
>
> - Genesis 39:7 (KJV)

I believe that the wife of Potiphar is a good example of a woman who is unable to control her appetite. Like today's "Desperate Housewives," she has a husband who is very successful in the world, but not taking care of business at home. Mrs. Potiphar's husband was one of the most powerful and successful men in Egypt. She had everything that a woman could desire, but she was not content with what she had because she felt as though she did not have him—he left her alone for long periods of time.

Her appetite for sex mixed with her desire for attention caused her to lust after Joseph, who was a slave boy in her household. Joseph was not anywhere near her level, but she had been checking him out and had decided that she wanted him. Similar to the way Esau sold his birthright, these emotions began not with his actions but with her thoughts. Potiphar's wife going after Joseph began with a thought that she did not control and dismiss.

When her appetite for sex was aroused, instead of fulfilling it with her husband, she began to wonder what it would be like to sleep with Joseph. Instead of using the appetite in the institution of marriage that had been provided to her, she looked for another outlet. What began as a fleeting thought became an obsession.

She eventually became overwhelmed with the thought that she should pursue him. That thought led to her actions, so she followed her passions and desires by seeking opportunities when her husband was absent to make advances to Joseph. She wanted her husband's attention, but was willing to accept Joseph's attention in his stead.

Please do not misunderstand what I am saying about Potiphar's wife. I am not saying that her appetite itself was evil. Although her appetite was not wrong; it was in fact a natural desire, but it was fueled by lust. The fact that her appetite led to her pursuit of a slave shows that when lust is ignited, it does not recognize the normal boundaries such as a person's class or station in life.

Although God had given her the desire and passion that she had, He gave it to her to be used within the context of her marriage. Lust twisted what was a natural desire into an ungodly passion. Because she was like any other woman, Potiphar wife's emotions were hard to hide. Eventually, her actions showed what she had been thinking and feeling.

The enemy will tempt you to get something through ungodly means that you already have or can already get through the channels that God has provided for you. If you are married and you have an appetite for sex, God has given you a husband to fulfill your needs.

The enemy will cleverly put someone else in front of you who may be younger, may look better than your spouse, and maybe even sound better. He will present you with someone more intelligent and articulate, who has a great voice that can melt even the stoniest of hearts. That is how he gets people to leave what they have been blessed with, in order to shift their focus and pursue what he tells them they can have.

The enemy deceives you, but you have to remember that as a believer, it is up to you to cultivate what you have. God will not present you with a finished product: a career that is already set up and ready for you to take over, or a relationship that is absolutely perfect. You have to work at making your life, what you and God desires it to be.

Much like the men, though for the ladies it is not every man that you are vulnerable to but it is just that one man. Ladies, you might think, *"Oh, I am not interested in other men, only my husband."* But then you say, *"Why can't my husband be more like him?"* Guard your thoughts and emotions toward every man who is not your husband; make the fear of God the first thought if the devil presents someone that appears better than your husband

FLEE IMMORALITY

> *"And it came to pass about this time, that Joseph went into the house to do his business; and there was none of the men of the house there within. And she caught him by his garment, saying, Lie with me: and he left his garment in her hand, and fled, and got him out."*
>
> - Genesis 39:11 & 12 (KJV)

Let us see what else the Bible has to say about what we need to do when confronted with a bad situation like Joseph:

> *"Flee Fornication. Every sin that a man doeth is without the body; but he that committeth fornication sinneth against his own body."*
>
> -1 Corinthians 6:18 (KJV)

> *"Flee also youthful lusts: but follow righteousness, faith, charity, peace, with them that call on the Lord out of a pure heart."*
>
> - 2 Timothy 2:22 (KJV)

> *"Submit yourselves therefore to God. Resist the devil and he will flee from you."*
>
> - James 4:27 (KJV)

Joseph's response was in accordance with the Bible; he ran away so fast that he left his coat in her hand. He did not care about his coat; rather he cared about his character. His response was *"how can I do this thing and sin against my God?"* His constant resistance stemmed from a reverence for God. He saw the situation for what it really was: sin. He did not say *"Sure"* and then *"Wait, no, I better not."* He just said *"No"* and ran.

Now consider the way Potiphar's wife dealt with her rejection. Although her appetite was not wrong, it was fueled with passion, enflamed with desire, directed at someone other than her husband, and she allowed it to continue to grow into lust.

Once you allow your appetite to grow until it has no boundaries, expect that you will find it more and more difficult to control, like a spoiled child allowed everything he/she wants. When you finally say *"no,"* you get mismanaged fury. Do not allow lust to come into your life and twist what God has given to you.

Potiphar's wife is unique in that she was using both the Jezebel spirit and the harlot spirit. She kept trying to wear Joseph down, but he remained strong in the faith and did not give into the temptation under any circumstances. When the Jezebel spirit did not work, she employed the harlot spirit. She made sure when all the men were gone; she tried to take advantage of Joseph's situation. When the opportune time came, she made her move.

When you are married, you already have a wife or a husband, but the devil tempts you with someone else. He begins to show you things you already have, but lets you look at it in a way that you do not recognize that you have it. If you look his way and see what he has to offer, you will be deceived into thinking it is something you do not already have in your possession. The devil ensnares us using a device, a sickness, a weakness, a habit, or generational curse; any tool available.

CHAPTER TEN

[WHAT ABOUT YOU?]

Many people don't understand the effects of sexual immorality because they don't fully know the dynamics of the sexual process. The man by nature and design is the projector and the woman by nature and design is the receptor. When sexual intercourse takes place, souls combine and oxytocin (the chemical that binds people together) is secreted. As a result, a DNA impression is taken and left with you. More information on this will be given shortly.

To many, this may seem arbitrary, but to those who understand the spiritual realm know this means open doors for spirits to enter and ruin your life. For those who have been sexually active you know once you have done it for the first time, your appetite for it is extremely heightened. It may take you six months in a relationship to have sex for the first time, but the second time, it may take two weeks because your life is now open to the act as well as the demons associated with fornication or adultery.

For this reason we advise those who have been sexually active before marriage to seek a series of counseling as well as deliverance sessions because some demons are harder to drive out than others. There is something we call the fragmented soul which is basically leaving part of your soul with each person you have sex with. Many people are walking around wounded and crushed as well as heavy laden because of this. Christ came to save our souls and our souls also need to be restored from this fragmentation.

When you examine a healthy marital relationship, the sexual intimacy between the two people creates powerful physical, emotional, and chemical changes in the body of each. It works as a narrowing process where their brains begin to focus in on each other facilitating more physical intimacy. In order for either partner in the marriage to climax, they must focus their attention on each other and block out all distractions.

The chemical and biological processes involved in the sexual act are:

- Dopamine: This chemical registers pleasure in the mind.

- Norepinephrine: This chemical gives your body a natural boost of adrenaline. It also increases memory capacity, helping to sear the experience into your memory.

- Testosterone: This hormone is known for creating sexual desire in both men and women. In men, especially, it creates feelings of positive energy and well-being.

- Oxytocin: This chemical flood the brain at climax and acts as a natural tranquilizer. It lowers blood pressure, blunts sensitivity to pain and stress, and induces sleep.

- Serotonin: This chemical is not released until immediately after climax. It creates a deep feeling of calmness, satisfaction and stress release.

When a husband and wife have sex, they move down this funnel together, which seals the bond between them. Although there is a physical and chemical experience, it is more than that: it is a joining of mind, spirit, and emotions, which is based upon the experiences they have had together.

Now, consider this process when a man and woman are not married. Although all of the same chemicals are released, they function differently. The dopamine focuses your attention on the experience and not the person. The norepinephrine induces the same adrenaline rush and takes a snapshot of the moment to store in your memory.

Testosterone increases your desire for more short term pleasure. Oxytocin makes you feel calm and sleepy. And Serotonin causes you to forget all your worries and troubles only to have them come rushing back with guilt once the process is complete. Another chemical might be released, that is part of the fight or flight response, known as Cortisol.

For what you are doing may put you at risk, your brain deals with it by pumping extra chemicals into your body that will intensify the effects of the other chemicals. This means that a temporary sexual experience will feel more intense and exciting, but it's only a trick.

The more you place yourself in that situation, the less your brain believes it's dangerous, and the fight or flight hormones stop being released. Once you have completed the process and tried to move on, the stored memory will only bring you guilt.

I reiterate here, apart from the biological implications, we must be careful who our friends are. We look at the Israelites and see that no matter how much it was attempted to curse them, God protected His own; He guarded them all the way. On the other hand, Balaam stepped in and befriended the people.

Your association with Christ choses some battles for you, but your association with some persons can inflict you with much more grief than you ever imagined. People often only look at the natural implications of unwanted pregnancies or sexually transmitted diseases, but there are sexual demons that are lurking for souls to inhabit.

In your life, it is also important to have someone to whom you are accountable. This person must not be a friend or colleague, who is equal to you in wisdom and experience. Instead, you must find a mentor; someone you respect and admire, and someone you are able to be honest and open with, in every area of your life; someone who has walked the path before and either obeyed the Word to the letter or made mistakes and grew from them.

You need someone who will lift you up in prayer, build you up in support and cheer you on as you grow. We can look again at Samson, who disregarded his parents' wishes. Instead of looking for a wife among his own people who worshipped the one true God, he went looking for a wife among his enemies. How would Samson be able to kill the Philistines if he married one of them?

Samson did not like the advice that did not agree with his own thoughts on the situation. His parents were wise to understand that marrying outside the faith was only going to bring about trouble, and they also knew that marrying someone from the Heathen City would only result in a bad alliance. More upsetting is that he had taken the Nazarite vow and was supposed to have set himself apart for service to the Lord.

Now, he wanted to break God's law by marrying someone who was not an Israelite. In fact, the woman had not even converted to believe in the one true God. Samson was forgetting his purpose, which was to bring judgment upon the Philistines. He was unique for his time and gifted in a way that few in the Scriptures were. You, likewise, are different than the unbelieving world around you because you are not of this world.

You need to stay away from the temptations of the Heathen City. You are called to be something special as well, for the Scripture speaks that we are a royal priesthood; salt of the earth. This is why we must not contaminate or defile our temples, especially in the area of sexual immorality. If he had an accountability partner, he/she could have reminded him of his call and guide him to stay on the path God mapped out for him.

Additionally, to stay sexually pure, as implied above, you will need a regular prayer life that fosters a constant deliberate relationship with God. At times the devil steps in when we are at our weakest. He knows when our prayer life, worship, Bible study and witness are lacking and will come at us to tempt us. You must be vigilant that you do not weaken the connection you have with God because that means you weaken your defenses against the enemy and hence he can get you to do whatever he wants.

To continue to resist the temptation of sexual sins, you will need a conscious and concentrated commitment to developing your character. You must be strong mentally, emotionally and socially is you are to live a victorious life, free of sexual impurities.

You will need a character like Joseph that dictates no matter what you consider how it will affect your relationship with God first. You will need a heart like David that knows when you make mistakes, you run to God and seek forgiveness, repent and ask for the grace to go forward. You will need a page out of Judah's book to focus on why you were created – for worship. And you will need strength like Samson, but an internal strength, not a physical strength only.

Some of you reading this book are called to bring deliverance to your families, homes, workplaces, schools, communities, nations. But you may have flaws like the men mentioned previously. It doesn't mean that you will make the same mistakes as they did; nor does it mean your destiny will end like theirs.

Anything that will draw your strength and cause you to be weak and separate you from God is forbidden. Some may seek sexual immorality because they are looking for a place to rest. But rest is not found there; you will lose more of your strength by laying your head in the lap of fornication. Samson had taken himself to a place where he should not have been and was planning on forming an alliance with a woman that he should have avoided.

So, on one hand we have the exceedingly strong Samson, who is the deliverer of God's people, and who has been as glorious in battle as the sun is during the breaking of day. On the other hand, we have Delilah, whose aim is to bring down this man, which was quite simple, since she and the other Philistine women are like kryptonite to Samson.

These are the type of people that the devil loves to target within the church; those who are doing or trying to do mighty things. He looks for their greatest flaws and can easily bring them down when they are weary and not looking for trouble. And he sends people like Delilah to pull them away from their God-ordained purpose, so the ones we stay close to must be following Christ as well and achieving great things for Him.

Sometimes it begins as a ministry to a member of the opposite sex. You think you can help them – it is your job to help them. Then you spend time with them and neglect your spouse. During this time, your spouse may show jealousy, which you think is unfounded. Then, before you know it, you have submitted to the sin and overruled boundaries.

Just as Samson was to be a light to others, we need to be lights shining in the darkness. We need to stay out of the darkness and keep ourselves from hiding secrets in the darkness. Like Samson, we may have character flaws in our own life. There may be some moral weakness that is keeping us from fully being what God wants us to be, and we need to address it.

We need to be so careful, because everything that our heart desires is not always the best thing for us. Samson was hurt, from the time of his first relationship with a woman, who betrayed him. Similarly, many of us make decisions based on past hurts. Have you ever been hurt by your own family or friends?

It is similar to what Joseph experienced in his own house from his brothers who sold him as a slave. But like Joseph, what the enemy meant for evil, God can turn it around to work for good. As leaders and believers, we have an obligation to remain pure. Sexual immorality is a sin. Whenever we break our vows, God's strength leaves us.

We cannot let our head be shaven, figuratively; otherwise the capacity in which God is using us can be compromised causing much shame and grief. Like Samson we get up and try to shake ourselves free from past times and memories. We want to function again based on past anointing, but we have severed our link with revelation. Our strength is gone.

Samson lost his strength, his integrity, his position, and his sight when the soldiers came in. He was then sentenced to do the work of an ox and turn the mill. In the end he was totally humiliated. From a mighty man of Zorah, he fell captive to the Philistines. From being bright like the sun, he became blind. Samson went from the glory of a warrior of God to being treated like a common work animal.

This book has opened your mind to the devices of the enemy and much more so you are equipped now to choose the right path or guard your path and ultimately your God-ordained purpose. In 1 Corinthians 6:18, Paul said that the sexual sin is a sin against one's own body. Any other sin that a person can commit takes place outside the body, but sexual sin allows defilement to enter your body.

Now, this might not seem like a big deal, until you realize that your body is supposed to be the temple of the Holy Spirit. Your body, as a believer, belongs to God. You are the church! It is a great victory for the enemy when he is able to get you to defile yourself by convincing you to do things that contaminate your temple; he is in effect contaminating the body of Christ. It also sabotages your mission on this earth.

It is important to note here that even if you have already fallen prey to sexual sins there is much hope for you. Once there is life, there is hope in Christ. But you need to tread lightly. What do I mean? You may have repented and feel ready for public ministry or pulpit ministry, but you need to complete your personal ministry. By this I refer to being fully healed and delivered first.

We know God forgives but every single action has consequences and there are things to be dealt with in our own lives, sometimes with others and sometimes in environments before you can be fully restored but it is very possible. Let God take His time and do a holistic cleansing in you before getting back into ministry.

You may also need to accept that you may never be ready to operate in the capacity you once did based on the extent of the damage done. You must stay strong and faithful; it doesn't mean that God cannot use you at all. In some cases, He may just shift you to working in a different capacity.

Get your house in order according to the saying. Work on yourself, your marriage (if you were married), and your mind before you get back into the ministry. You will have to fight a heated battle on multiple fronts. Keep in mind that once you have fallen, the devil knows just how to chase you in a way to make you susceptible to the same sin again.

If you do not step back and wait out of the spotlight of spiritual warfare, then you will end up stuck back in the same pattern of error that you were once in. If you have not properly grown out of the experience, you may be setting yourself up for another fall. Seek the guidance and evaluations of mentors and accountability partners because if you rush back in and sin again, you will do no good for yourself or for God's ministry.

One last area I must shed a little light on is sexual impurities with one's self. When viewing pornography, your body still releases all these chemicals, but you focus your attention and develop your attachment to pictures or videos; fictional characters are your muse. The viewer is prone to use the pornography as an escape from reality in the same way as a drug user or an alcoholic.

The memories that are stored are photos or actions and the desire that is increased is for more pornography. Like the 'fling', the images viewed conflict with the conscience. They also move at a quicker rate that what the brain can process. This means that the viewer releases an abundance of cortisol and boosts their hormone levels higher.

Likewise, masturbation is forbidden for the believer because it damages one's perception and expectation of the sexual encounter. Masturbation is the act of pleasuring one's self; it is a highly selfish act that goes against the Word of God, which admonishes us to deny ourselves daily (Luke 9:23). Masturbation in fact causes one to begin to believe he/she doesn't need anyone else to be gratified sexually.

Some say it's better than pre-marital sex or adultery, but it ranks on the same scale as all other forms of sexual perversion. If God felt that masturbation was a viable sexual option, He would never have created Eve with a reproductive organ perfectly designed to host and bring pleasure to Adam's reproductive organ. It is important for us to see masturbation for what it truly is – a sin.

As with any drug, the brain becomes desensitized and need to sink deeper into perversion to obtain the same high or risk boredom. When a couple is in a healthy marriage relationship, they share experiences and as the relationship progresses it changes daily through these experiences. This makes each act of sexual intimacy new and unique and keeps the excitement alive.

However, when a person has a one-time sexual encounter, few experiences are shared, if the person is not new or different the brain begins to see each encounter as the same. Once the act is over, the chemicals dissipate and the sensation is gone. Then rational thinking returns and causes the person to realize the extent of his/her actions. The loss of the thought process during the act comes back to haunt him/her.

Once rational thinking is working again, there is no way to erase the event. Maybe you already have a secret. Maybe no one has figured it out and they think you are so holy. It keeps gnawing at you in the back of your brain: that one time you gave in to your urges.

It is indeed a daily struggle. You struggle to not give in or not give in again and you struggled with the times in the past when you did give in and all this struggling is done alone because you do not want anyone to know your secret for obvious reasons. Truth is, when you keep your secret in the darkness, the prince of darkness has control over it.

The devil is a liar and when you expose him and you open your secret up for the Holy Spirit to come inside and cleanse it, and then it can begin to get better. God can deal with things that people cannot and darkness loses its power when you hand it over to Him.

When we look at the mighty men who have fallen into sexual impurity, we see that they all had to suffer some sort of discipline. Thankfully, at some point after they returned to God, they were led back to their position. Samson was even led by a small child and positioned between the pillars, so he could complete his work. God may use little things in your life, too.

God's mercy and grace work together in your life to answer your prayers and relieve the burden from your shoulders. Just keep in mind – Samson asked God for the strength to do His will and although he got his request, he died in the process. The guiding principle is that once you fall from your position, nothing will make it the same again.

Once David fell from his close relationship with God, he had to experience family struggles and the death of a child. Even after he died, his sins fell onto his sons, notably Solomon. Samson never recovered his sight. Tamar got a child, but never a husband. Remember this when you are going through times of restoration and recovery.

Frequently, you may feel on top of the world now that your soul has been lifted from the burden of your secret. You may want to rush out and return to the ministry so you can begin to help others. You may feel strong and ready to take on anything. But you need to relax and let God complete His work in you.

It's too common that people return to the ministry close on the heels of a sexual sin. They have the guilt removed and they are ready to take on the world. But the harlot spirits do not like to give up their victims easily and the devil still has a hit out on your life.

So you feel strong enough to take on the world? Samson was strong. So you are devoted to God? David was devoted to God. So you only want one thing – just to return to ministry? Tamar only wanted one thing. Are you to the point where you would do anything to prove you are ready to get back into the ministry? Esau was ready to do anything, just so he could get a taste of Jacob's stew.

God may have restored your strength, but he has not restored your sight. If you do not sit and wait on the sidelines, the same sin that messed you up before can mess you up again. You are strong, but you are still blind. God does not want you to go back into the battle until you can see the enemy.

ROTA - SEX IN THE CITY

PRACTICAL GUIDELINES

OPEN YOUR EYES

Every time there is sexual impurity among the leaders or congregants, there are obvious manifestations which we need to pay attention to. Always be on the lookout for signs. Marked changes in behavior don't occur overnight so one must be vigilant and when these signs show up, take the necessary steps to address the situation.

COME CLEAN

It never helps to cover up sin, but to address it. Any rehabilitation agency will tell us that 'admitting it is always the beginning of the recovery' process. Secrecy is often the devil's way of keeping people bound to sin. Making the sin public is not humiliation, its strength as it provides an opportunity for forgiveness and restoration.

NO EXCUSES

Many times we want to make excuses for sin under the guise of not condemning people but sexual perversion is a serious sin that must be handled immediately and forcefully. More often than not, people feel they can get away with this folly when excuses can be conjured.

PARTNER UP

Having an accountability partner is one of the safest ways to avoid sexual sins. Of course he/she must be trustworthy and willing to walk along the path with you. You will need someone calling you at all hours of the night, checking up on you during a date, etc. But it is better to be safe than sorry.

SENTRY DUTY

This is precisely how we are to be with our praise – always on guard. Sexual impurity almost always affects the praise of the house. This is no surprise since this is the way the church connects with God. So as long as there is sin, it will have a bearing on the church's relationship with God and hence their worship. Sin in a house rises as a stench to God.

BAGGAGE

Newton's Third Law that states "every action has an equal and opposite reaction" is simply a by-product of the Bible. The Bible puts it this way "For the one who sows to his own flesh shall from the flesh reap corruption, but the one who sows to the Spirit shall from the Spirit reap eternal life." (Galatians 6:7&8) We see in the lives of David and Samson and a host of other Bible characters how their sins had consequences. God always forgives our sins, but we remain with its effects.

LOOK TO THE STRIPPER

As much as it may seem hopeless in the midst of the scourge of this sin, God can and will restore if hearts become sincere towards Him. There must be genuine repentance for God to begin the process and thus complete it. It will take time because of the outcome of this sin, often times, resulting in broken homes, illegitimate children, the contraction of various diseases and even death. Patiently, give God the time and space He needs to do His work because He always does His best.

LEARN SUBJECTION

We must daily put our flesh under the subjection of the Spirit. Throughout the Bible we see the war between Flesh and Spirit, but once we have mastered the art of subjecting our flesh, we will live a more fulfilling, victorious life in Christ. Die daily to the inner desires that plague you. Train your mind to respond only to what the Spirit urges and not the carnal tugs of the human heart.

THE END

NOTES:

NOTES:

NOTES:

NOTES:

Made in the USA
Charleston, SC
09 July 2015